Resources in Education

Teaching Science in the Primary School

Book One:
A Practical Source Book of Teaching Strategies

Edited by
Alan Cross and Gill Peet

Northcote House

ISBN 0 7463 0679 2

British Library Cataloguing-in-Publication Data
A catalogue record for this book is available
from the British Library

First published in 1997 by Northcote House Publishers Ltd,
Plymbridge House, Estover Road, Plymouth PL6 7PY,
United Kingdom.
Tel: Plymouth (01752) 202368. Fax: (01752) 202330.

Typeset by Kestrel Data, Exeter
Printed and bound in Great Britain

Contents

Notes on Contributors   7

PART 1. The Context: Background to Primary Science

1 Keeping Science at the Core   15
Alan Cross and Gill Peet

2 Children Learning in Science   24
Linda McGuigan and Mike Schilling

3 Language and Learning in Science   37
David Heywood

PART 2. Issues of Quality in Provision

4 Progression in Learning in Science   51
Stuart Naylor and Brenda Keogh

5 Differentiation in Teaching Science   64
Stuart Naylor and Brenda Keogh

6 Equal Opportunities and the Teaching of Science   76
Gill Peet

7 Science in the Early Years   93
Karen Hardy and Chris Macro

8 Science 1   106
David Byrne

9 Assessment and Recording as a Constructive
   Process   122
Ron Ritchie

10 Information Technology as Essential in Primary
    Science   135
Alan Cross

11 Cross-Curricular Links in Science   152
Carole Naylor and Anthony Pickford

12 Home–School Links in Science   169
Conrad Chapman

PART 3. Managing Primary Science

13 The Role of the Co-ordinator   185
Gill Peet

14 The Monitoring and Evaluation of Science in the
    Primary School   198
Alan Cross and Alan Chin

Index   212

Notes On Contributors

EDITORS

Alan Cross

Alan has taught both infants and juniors as a class teacher and deputy headteacher. Later he led Salford LEA's Primary Science and Technology Unit for three years. Presently he is Lecturer in Primary Education at the Department of Education, University of Manchester. He now leads both the science and the design and technology elements on the one-year PGCE primary course. He runs short courses for primary teachers, leads development and evaluation projects and has addressed a number of overseas international conferences. He has written widely in the areas of science, technology and information technology including *Design and Technology 5–11* published by Hodder and Stoughton. Currently Alan is researching teaching styles in primary design and technology.

Gill Peet

Gill is an experienced class teacher of both infants and juniors and taught for a number of years in a multi-racial primary school. She worked formerly as an advisory teacher for primary science and technology and is currently a senior lecturer at Manchester Metropolitan University where she is responsible for co-ordinating the science in education course for B.Ed students. She also teaches design and technology. Gill has led many INSET sessions, including 20-day science courses. She has recently conducted research into children's investigations in science and has published in the area of equal opportunities. She is an Ofsted-trained Inspector.

BACKGROUND OF WRITERS

David Byrne

David acts as a consultant to LEAs and schools and is an Ofsted-trained Inspector. He has published widely, including materials for Lego Dacta, five titles for the Longmans Book Project, the BP science-based resource, *Living with Traffic*, and the Teacher Time-savers Publication *Physical Processes*. David is a regular contributor to both *Junior* and *Child Education* magazines. He has had over 25 years experience in primary education in both Britain and abroad. He has taught across the 5–11 range and has held posts of responsibility for science in two large urban primary schools. In 1985 he took up the post of Teacher Adviser where he co-ordinated a team of advisory teachers supporting primary schools in science and technology in Bury LEA. This involved the delivery of a range of courses both regionally and nationally. In 1992 he took up the post of Course Leader of the Science B.Ed (Hons) Department at the North East Wales Institute of Higher Education. David works as a freelance educational writer, inspector and consultant.

Conrad Chapman
Conrad is the head of a multi-cultural, multi-racial community school in Oldham (Greenhill Community School). He was the first co-ordinator of the Royal Society of Arts (RSA) Home-School Contract of Partnership Project and is currently a part-time INSET provider and lecturer at Manchester University's School of Education. His more recent publications in the home-school sphere include *Home–School Work in Britain* and *A Willing Partnership*.

Alan Chin
Alan is an experienced primary school teacher and is currently deputy headteacher of Ludworth Primary School in Stockport where he has specific responsibility for science and whole-school curriculum development. In the areas of science education, Alan has given support to initial teacher training students at both Manchester University and Manchester Metropolitan University. He has also been involved in providing INSET to serving teachers, on the role of the science co-ordinator in the inspection process, and to deputy head-teachers on aspects of management. Currently Alan is working with the Manchester Museum of Science and Industry in the development of support materials for their exhibits.

Karen Hartley
Karen has had many years experience as a teacher of young children. Before becoming an advisory teacher for science she was deputy headteacher of a primary school with responsibility for the infant

department. Whilst working as an advisory teacher she was involved in the SPACE research undertaken by CRIPSAT at Liverpool University. She is an endorsed trainer of the High Scope approach to the development of young children's teaching and is co-author of teaching materials for primary science. She is presently employed as a senior lecturer at Edge Hill College of Higher Education where she teaches on the BA, BSc and QTS courses and is an INSET provider on both award-bearing and short courses.

David Heywood

David is a senior lecturer in the Department of Sciences Education at the Manchester Metropolitan University. He works on initial teacher training courses and co-ordinates the primary INSET programme including GEST-funded 10- and 20-day science courses for primary teachers. He has worked in several primary schools as a co-ordinator for both science and technology. His current research interest is in the field of language and interpretation of scientific ideas. A former advisory teacher in science and technology, he has experience of working in both primary schools and secondary schools. Prior to his present position, David was deputy headteacher of a large primary school.

Brenda Keogh

Brenda is currently senior lecturer at Manchester Metropolitan University where she is involved in initial and in-service education. Presently Brenda directs Streamwatch UK, a national environmental project. Prior to this, she taught mainly in primary schools and worked as an advisory teacher and National Curriculum Co-ordinator. She is involved in the work of the Association for Science Education and the British Association. Her professional interests are mostly shared with her husband Stuart Naylor, and include teacher professional development, public access to science and the connection between teaching and learning. Her most recent publication is *Scientists and Primary Schools: a Practical Guide*, which outlines an innovative approach to learning science through concept cartoons.

Linda McGuigan

Linda taught primary children in Lancashire from 1986 to 1989. She worked as a teacher fellow and later as a research associate at the Centre for Research in Primary Science and Technology, University of Liverpool, from 1989 to 1995. Linda was a member of the SPACE Project team which explored children's understanding of science and co-authored the Nuffield Primary Science curriculum materials. Between 1991 and 1994 she was involved in an evaluation of the implementation of National Curriculum science Key Stage 1 to Key Stage 3 for SCAA. Since 1995 she has worked as a lecturer at the University of Warwick contributing to the initial teacher education programme.

Chris Macro
Chris taught for many years in primary schools and for five years led the Primary Science and Technology initiative in St Helens LEA. She was for a time a member of CRIPSAT at the University of Liverpool and was co-author of teacher training materials for science education. Chris has had a number of short articles published and is presently conducting research into the use of information technology in science education. She works at Edge Hill College of Higher Education where, as senior lecturer, she teaches in the Primary Science department. Chris provides INSET on both short and award-bearing courses and acts as an educational consultant.

Carole Naylor
Carole worked as a class teacher in primary schools for a number of years before joining Manchester LEA's team for primary science and technology. Since 1988 she has worked at University College, Chester where as a senior lecturer and section leader for Science works on courses of initial teacher education.

Stuart Naylor
Stuart is currently principal lecturer at Manchester Metropolitan University where he is involved in initial and in-service teacher education. Prior to this he taught mainly in secondary schools in this country and the USA and worked as an advisory teacher. He is involved in the work of the Association for Science Education and the British Association. His professional interests are mostly shared with his wife Brenda Keogh, and include teacher professional development, public access to science and the connection between teaching and learning. His most recent publication is *Scientists and Primary Schools: a Practical Guide*, which outlines an innovative approach to learning science through concept cartoons.

Tony Pickford
After sixteen years as a primary class teacher in Tameside, Tony moved to University College Chester in 1990 to teach on the B.Ed

and PGCE (Primary) programmes. He now teaches in both the technology and teacher education departments on a range of modules. Tony has published articles in several journals, including *Primary Science Review* and the *British Journal of Educational Technology*. Tony is also IT co-ordinator for the School of Education.

Ron Ritchie

Ron is Head of the Department for Professional Development at Bath College of Higher Education and teaches on initial and in-service education programmes. Ron has taught in primary and secondary schools and was an advisory teacher for primary science in Avon. He is author of books and articles on the teaching of science and technology including *Primary Science: Making it Work* (with Chris Ollerenshaw) (1997), and *Primary Design and Technology: a Process for Learning* (1995) both published by David Fulton. He has been involved in several research projects in science, one of which focused on assessment and was funded by the National Primary Centre. Before working in higher education he taught in primary schools.

Mike Schilling

Mike taught primary children in Leicestershire from 1978 to 1984. He worked as primary science tutor with PGCE students at the University of Leicestershire from 1984 to 1987 and has been Deputy Director of the Centre for Research in Primary Science and Technology (CRIPSAT) at the University of Liverpool (Department of Education) since 1987. He ran DES-designated 20-day courses in primary science from 1990 to 1992 and has been Project Manager for the Key Stage 2 Standard Tests in Science Project (funded by SEAC/SCAA) since 1992.

PART 1

The Context:
Background to Primary Science

1
Keeping Science at the Core

Alan Cross and Gill Peet

INTRODUCTION

This book is intended to provide a sound basis for the teaching of science to children in Key Stages 1 and 2. The accompanying book (*Teaching Science in the Primary School: Book 2: An Action Pack for Primary Teachers*) will take readers a step further in terms of implementing the recommendations of the first book. In this book the various authors have been careful to adopt a practical approach. They have concentrated their attention on the classroom, on teaching and on children, and address all those concerned with developing primary science. Key issues are dealt with which relate to the teaching and learning processes in science, the use of language, the role of the science co-ordinator, resourcing, monitoring and evaluation. This book will be useful for class teachers, students training to be primary teachers, university tutors, inspectors and advisory teachers. There will also be considerable value in the book for lay people including parents, lay inspectors and school governors.

WHY DO WE WANT PRIMARY CHILDREN TO DO SCIENCE?

Science helps children to understand more about their world. They are naturally curious and so a major aim of science education is to stimulate and develop this curiosity. Science, however, is not simply a matter of teaching children facts or giving answers to their questions, but is about allowing children the opportunity to develop the skills to find out for themselves and to go on raising questions and looking for answers throughout their lives. In this way they will be prepared as citizens of a democratic society, who collectively have enormous power to approve or disapprove of 'scientific' developments that might pollute or preserve our planet or affect the quality of life for the citizens of the planet. As the human population increases and for some within that population personal wealth increases, it is increasingly important that all individuals see how science fits into their lives. In 1985 the *Science 5-16: A Statement of Policy (DES, 1985)*, recognised that:

> Each of us needs to be able to bring a scientific approach to bear on the practical, economic and political issues of modern life.
>
> (para. 7)

Such preparation for life is best begun in the early years.

The challenge of science in compulsory education 5-16 and particularly in the primary years 4-11 is about opportunity and quality.

> We need to ask what kind of science education for the ordinary pupil will lead to a scientific literacy which would form the basis of an informed public opinion capable of understanding at least in some degree what scientists are doing.
>
> (Ingle and Jennings, 1981, p.75)

All children can do science, all children can be successful in science (Cross and Pearce, 1993), but to answer the question 'what kind of science?' we need to have a view of the nature of science itself.

Science in the primary years is a practical subject which is often associated with answers. However, at the heart of science we find questions. Great scientists of history are noted for the so-called 'answers' they found (for example, Darwin's explanation of the diversity of living things in his theory of evolution) or for those things they discovered (for example, Curie's discovery of Radium). Curie's discovery took humankind another small step along the road of knowledge and understanding, as did a powerful concept like that of Darwin's. However, even concepts or ideas such as these are only good until a better one comes along. Scientists were once convinced that the earth was at the centre of the universe and that the stars rotated around it. In the sixteenth century Nicolaus Copernicus (1473-1543) offered a better model which was based on the sun being at the centre of the universe and the earth and other heavenly bodies orbiting the sun. The scientific and religious community took some time to accept this new idea but other scientists were later to improve on the Copernican model and we now have widely accepted theories or explanations of planetary motion which we call 'scientific'. They are, however, like all scientific theories, only provisional. That is, although we have lots of observations which do not refute them, it may be that in time another scientist might propose alternative theories (Popper, 1988). For example, it was Aristotle's scientific theory that objects would fall at speeds proportional to their weight. This idea was held for more than 2000 years before Newton was able to prove it to be false. When this occurs we have a new scientific theory (see Hawking, 1988 for a readable discussion). It is in this way that science progresses, and no generation can be said to have all of the 'answers'! Theories of science are not fixed but evolve as they are refined through the discovery of new or conflicting evidence. This realisation can be very difficult to those of us living in a world where scientists are almost always sought to solve human problems.

Questions are at the heart of this very practical subject we call science. Only those of us able to ask questions are in a position to seek answers. Importantly, there are scientific skills and there is scientific knowledge which, when available to the individual, allow that individual more effectively to seek solutions or answers.

We all appear to start our lives able and confident to explore; time spent with a baby or young infant should convince us of that. Whilst humans appear to become more sophisticated, this basic desire to enquire and to seek explanations seems to stay with most of us, although experience affects our attitudes and influences those areas in which we are happy to investigate. For example, there is a considerable body of research (Browne, 1991) to show that girls often develop a negative attitude towards science and the possible role in science for females. This and other negative attitudes to science can be formed at an early age. Another example is the commonly held view that science is considered as suitable only for 'academic' individuals. Primary education can reinforce this if the most articulate children continually receive praise for their work and other children who might be far more inventive are perhaps discouraged solely because they lack the vocabulary to express themselves clearly. Bilingual children often fall into this category. It might be worth noting that Isaac Newton did not attend school.

Language is very much tied up with science and scientific investigation. Language is required to articulate and explain and so science is constantly developing its language to cope with its new discoveries; for example, protons, quarks, charm, etc. If you do not know the word or if your language lacks a word for a concept it is difficult to deal with that concept and in this way barriers are created or reinforced. Scientists sometimes appear to be guilty of surrounding themselves in this specialist vocabulary and one problem that teachers experience is that they themselves, like other adults, are often confused by 'scientific' words. In such cases it seems inevitable that some of this confusion will be passed on to the children. A good example are the words we use to describe the everyday mixtures we make in the kitchen. When salt and water are mixed at room temperature they chemically combine to form a new substance, a *solution* we call brine. When sand is mixed with water it forms a *suspension*. In the latter case both the sand and the water remain chemically unchanged and the sand is 'suspended' in the water. Non-specialist primary teachers might use neither word or they might confuse them.

This area is related very much to the question of 'alternative understandings' which we all appear to hold. These ideas are 'alternative' because they do not match exactly the current 'scientific' understanding. An example relates to the cause of day and night. Sometimes when adults are interviewed, they explain the occurrence of day and night by explaining that the earth is still and the sun rotates around it! Only when they are asked to draw their idea and explain do they realise that it is to do with the spinning of the earth. When adults and children were asked to explain how light travels, some referred to 'waves', others to 'beams' or 'rays' of light, others to 'particles', and some to a kind of 'background' light which is just there (Driver, Guesne and Tiberghein, 1985). Research during the latter part of this century shows that we all have some of these 'mis-understandings' or misconceptions about currently held scientific concepts. This includes scientists unable to give the scientific explanation of a variety of concepts (Gunstone and Watts, 1985).

The authors have, in this book, attempted to consider some of these issues and in particular the debate about the relative weight which should be given, when teaching, to the processes of science and to the element of knowledge and understanding. This has been and continues to be a source of some tension for some primary teachers. A recurring theme throughout this book is the importance of the processes of science in developing knowledge and understanding.

CHALLENGES

Primary schools have made a considerable leap (Goldsworthy, 1995) in the years since the introduction of science within the National Curriculum in 1989 (DES, 1989). Despite this there remains considerable work to be done. In 1995 in their annual review following visits to school by Her Majesty's Inspectors and teams of Ofsted Inspectors, HMI reported the following key issues for primary schools (Ofsted, 1995):

- Steps need to be taken to enhance the science subject knowledge of teachers, especially those teaching older Key Stage 2 classes.

- Appropriate strategies should be developed for assessing pupils' progress in scientific knowledge and skills, and for ensuring the standardisation of the judgements of different teachers.

- Whole-school curriculum planning for science needs to be more systematic to ensure that all pupils have appropriate access to the full programme of study.

- Teaching in Key Stage 2 needs to be built more effectively on pupils' experience and achievement at Key Stage 1.

- Science co-ordinators need sufficient non-teaching time to develop their role more fully, including the monitoring of science teaching throughout the school.

There is discussion about the role of specialist teachers in UK primary schools. Some schools have opted for some form of specialist teaching in the upper junior years but for many schools such an option does not exist as they do not have a specialist in science on the school staff. In other primary schools there remains a strong commitment to the effective support of generalist class teachers by a subject co-ordinator and/or a specialist.

In examining these and other challenges the book has been divided into three parts. Part 1 – The Context: Background to Primary Science contains three chapters spelling out principles which are the foundation of good practice as it is presently perceived. The main part of the book is Part 2 – Issues of Quality in Provision, which turns attention to the various headings which all teachers must address to develop the subject. Finally, the shorter Part 3 has as its focus Managing Primary Science which, whilst not the main theme of the book, is so important if science is going to develop as a subject in the primary years. Teachers need to work at improving achievement in children's science in an environment which is supportive. The school must therefore provide leadership as well as resources and policy etc. so that teachers can focus their energies on the children.

STRATEGIES

Not all strategies will suit every school or every teacher. The writers in this book have all, in their careers, had to address the real problems of science teaching in primary classrooms. In their writing here they have taken a realistic approach. They have all identified challenges, outlined strategies to address them and importantly considered evaluation. While evaluation will go on all the time it is useful to set time aside for it and approach it in a systematic way so that you can make some judgement about how well your strategies are working. Because the authors have provided a number of strategies there should be an alternative if the reader finds that an approach does not appear to be effective for them.

This enquiring approach for professionals matches the enquiring approach in science. Such an approach permeates this book. It is most productive for teachers to challenge their personal ideas in science. This is emphasised in Part 1 where firstly McGuigan and Schilling spell out the dangers of ignoring the ideas that young children hold and point to constructivist approaches which build from the individual's understanding of the world. Science teaching is seen as a dialogue about scientific concepts between the children, the children and the teacher, and a personal dialogue that individuals can conduct with themselves. Wynne Harlen stresses the importance of such discussion with others:

> We have all probably had the experience where talking to someone has resulted in developing our own understanding, although apparently nothing was taken from the other person in terms of ideas. (Harlen, 1993, p.100)

In Chapter 3 David Heywood considers the important place of language in the development of ideas in science. His examples of exploring the concept of floating with young children will strike chords with experienced teachers. His additional example relating to the orbit of the moon may challenge the scientific understanding of readers (this may be an important step along the road for you!) to the point where you begin to ask questions about your own scientific understanding.

The second part of the book identifies areas which affect the quality of the science teaching and learning which will in turn affect the standards of children's achievement in science. There is a question as to whether we should assess this achievement on a narrow range of criteria, ie national assessment scores, or whether we might take a more holistic view. In Chapter 9 Ron Ritchie argues for a realistic and effective approach to assessment which is built upon the constructivist view that the teacher needs to know about the child's understanding of science in order to assist the child to move on. Assessment becomes more than completing tests, tasks or tick sheets, and finds its rightful place as part of the teaching process.

By asking Stuart Naylor and Brenda Keogh to contribute separate chapters on progression and differentiation the book emphasises the important contribution to furthering high standards of achievement in science. Teachers who have gone to the trouble of finding out or eliciting children's ideas about scientific phenomena are in a position to differentiate. Such differentiation if planned with care is very likely to lead to progression in that concepts will be developed. Stuart and Brenda have approached these areas pragmatically. They understand the pressure on primary teachers to teach nine subjects and more. They offer strategies which will be usable by all classroom teachers, not just those who happen to have relatively small classes.

With considerable emphasis on the development of scientific understanding and knowledge, David Byrne provides balance in his examination of the place of the scientific process in science. He argues that research into how children learn (Harlen, 1992) shows that the development of understanding is dependent on the ability to carry out process skills in a scientific manner and discusses ways in which teachers might approach this in their teaching.

Primary class teachers have, in the main, to teach all of the curriculum to their class. Their ability to do this has been and remains an area of debate (Alexander, Rose and Woodhead, 1992). Where this debate is balanced there is recognition of the strengths of cross-curricular approaches. Such approaches in the form of cross-curricular dimensions are written into the language of the National Curriculum (NCC, 1989). Naylor and Pickford stress how linking science to other areas of the curriculum can ensure that science is placed firmly in the context of the child's everyday experience of the world.

In Chapter 6 Gill Peet discusses equal opportunities and stresses how our Eurocentric view of science can help to develop stereotyped images which can work to devalue the contributions from other cultures. She asks how many black or women scientists can you name or how many inventions do you know that come from non-European or Black countries? She points out that if we consider how many pupils are underachieving in science because of unequal opportunities created by their culture, class or disability we are left with a small minority of scientifically literate people.

21

Karen Hartley and Chris Macro give us very clear exemplification of good practice in the early years with emphasis on the subject knowledge appropriate to teachers. They recognise the importance of both play and language acquisition in developing scientific awareness and their conclusions and strategies offered will be useful to teachers of all age ranges.

It is teachers of the early years who often have the most effective links with parents. This is usually based on the fact that parents of infants accompany the children to school. Thus teachers can use the opportunity for dialogue and the establishment of sound teacher-parent relationships. Conrad Chapman brings a huge amount of experience to this area. He reviews the movement that has seen so many primary schools foster home-school relations with very concrete outcomes in terms of learning. He shows that approaches used in areas like reading can be easily adapted to promote scientific learning. He gives us a real flavour of the potential for this interaction to benefit broad areas of learning and school life.

This part also includes an examination by Alan Cross of the potential offered to science in the primary years by information technology. That IT has a place in science ought not to be in doubt, but its place in science education is not so clear. A range of software applications are considered within a framework which covers most areas of potential. We still have some way to go in seeing this potential developed. This is linked in some measure to the development of suitable software, as well as the issue of access to computers. He recognises that with limited access it is difficult if not impossible to achieve all that we might wish to.

In the final part of the book Gill Peet exemplifies and discusses the role identified earlier, in the Ofsted report, of science co-ordinator. This role is at the heart of the development of the subject in primary schools. It is hard to conceive of a situation where some such role is not fulfilled. The exact nature of the role will depend on the headteacher, the school situation and of course the individual co-ordinator. You will need to consider the role carefully whether you are a science co-ordinator or likely to become one or you are a teacher who will need to relate to the science co-ordinator.

EVALUATION

It may be that had this book been written four or more years ago the final chapter might not have appeared. It might have been subsumed as one paragraph in the previous chapter, but we now have a situation where schools are being very publicly scrutinised. Thus it is necessary for schools to plan carefully for inspections. This is dealt with in Chapter 14 where Alan Cross and Alan Chin consider the monitoring of science. There are useful suggestions here that will have implications for preparation for school inspection but will also make the role of the co-ordinator clearer when identifying needs and preparing an action plan to deal with those needs.

Evaluation must always be in terms of the enrichment of the children's experiences and the improvement in their skills, knowledge, understanding and attitudes. This book is an attempt to help you think about what factors influence such improvement. Book 2 will provide further practical advice on how ideas might be translated into reality.

BIBLIOGRAPHY

Alexander, R., Rose, J. and Woodhead, C. (1992) *Curriculum Organisation and Classroom Practice in Primary Schools*. London: DES.

Browne, N. (ed.) (1991) *Science and Technology in the Early Years*. Milton Keynes: Open University Press.

Cross, A. and Pearce, G. (1993) Core Subject: Science, in P. Pumphery and G. Verma (eds) *Cultural Diversity and the Curriculum Volume 3, The Foundation Subjects and Religious Education in Primary Schools*. London: The Falmer Press.

DES (1985) *Science 5–16: A Statement of Policy*. London: HMSO.

DES (1989) *Science in the National Curriculum*. London: HMSO.

Driver, R., Guesne, E. and Tiberghein, A. (eds) (1985) *Children's Ideas in Science*. Buckingham: Open University Press.

Goldsworthy, A. (1995) Forces at Play on the Training Ground. *Times Educational Supplement*, Sept. 1995, Science Extra, p. 4.

Gunstone, R. and Watts, M. (1985) Force and Motion, in Driver, Guesne and Tiberghein, *op. cit.*

Harlen, W. (1992) *The Teaching of Science*. London: David Fulton.

Harlen, W. (1993) *Teaching and Learning in Primary Science*. London: Paul Chapman Publishing.

Hawking, S. (1988) *A Brief History of Time*. London: Bantam Press.

Ingle, R. and Jennings, A. (1981) *Science in Schools: Which Way Now?* Heinemann: London.

National Curriculum Council (NCC) (1989) *Curriculum Guidance: One – The Whole Curriculum*. York: NCC.

Ofsted (1995) *Science, A Review of Inspection Findings 1993/94*. London: HMSO.

Popper, K. (1988) Science: Conjectures and Refutations, in *Introductory Reading in the Philosophy of Science*. New York: Prometheus Books.

2
Children Learning in Science

Linda McGuigan and Mike Schilling

INTRODUCTION – EFFECTIVE LEARNING IN SCIENCE

A 'constructivist' approach to teaching children requires that they are enabled to build on existing ideas with new ideas which result from or are 'constructed' by new experiences:

> I didn't know my children had these ideas, it was a real eye opener. Ideas were coming thick and fast and I didn't know how to respond to them.

This teacher describes her feelings about her first attempts to implement a teaching approach which is sensitive to constructivist explanations of children's learning. The comment indicates her unfamiliarity with the range of ideas held by children. She implies that her former approach would have neglected such ideas. She also seems to suggest that she experienced some uncertainty in deciding how she could address such ideas in her classroom.

Active learning

Such a comment is typical of teachers' early experiences of implementing a constructivist approach to teaching and learning. This approach emphasises the role of the learner in constructing knowledge from existing ideas and from new information and experiences provided by the teacher. The learner is actively involved in the learning process, not simply by completing tasks imposed by the teacher or by absorbing information presented by the teacher but by engaging in activities which the teacher has designed as taking account of and as being an appropriate response to the child's developing understanding.

This view of the learner as being actively involved in the learning process has implications for the role of the teacher. Teachers will, for example, need to consider how children's ideas might be elicited in a classroom context and how they might most appropriately respond to children's ideas, as they emerge. Teachers will increasingly require a familiarity with the nature of children's progress within different areas of understanding in science. Teachers' own understanding of science may become a focus of concern as they implement the requirements of a National Curriculum using a constructivist approach.

This chapter briefly reviews constructivist approaches to science education, describes ways of eliciting children's ideas and offers some insights into how teachers might develop a repertoire of strategies which will help them to respond more appropriately to children's developing understanding in science. The final section briefly summarises the implications of adopting a constructivist approach.

CHALLENGES – CONSTRUCTIVISM IN SCIENCE EDUCATION

There has been a growing international interest in children's ideas about different areas of science understanding. Research papers have documented children's ideas in a variety of science concept areas (see Pfundt and Duit, 1994). Children's ideas often differ from the conventional science view. For instance, many young children claim that inanimate objects such as the sun and water are 'living' or 'alive' (Russell et al, forthcoming); some children consider solids to be strong, heavy materials and will tend not to regard powders or malleable materials as 'solid' (Russell et al, 1991).

When children hold views which differ from conventional scientific explanations or classifications, they are often referred to as 'misconceptions', 'alternative conceptions' or 'children's ideas'. However, the prevalence of these ideas is not restricted to children. Research has shown that adults share many of these views. While the origins of children's beliefs are uncertain, they are thought to have been formed as a result of previous experiences. For instance, some children describe the evaporation of water from a puddle as the water 'disappearing' (Russell and Watt, 1990). Some are influenced by folklore or the media. The ideas have a coherence; they make sense and seem to be useful in explaining children's own experiences of everyday phenomena. Furthermore, since ideas of this kind are intuitive and fruitful for children, they are resistant to change.

Recent constructivist ideas about teaching and learning (Harlen, 1993; *Background to Primary Science*) have been influenced to a great extent by earlier learning theorists such as Piaget (1970) and Vygotsky (1978), who believed that new learning is an interaction between the ideas children currently hold and newly presented experiences of information. Although constructivism is a broad term giving rise to a range of interpretations about how teachers should respond to children's ideas, nevertheless, there is a measure of agreement that children are not the passive recipients of knowledge but that conceptual development involves the active construction of new knowledge, a process which produces a change in ideas. There is agreement that the ideas children bring with them to science lessons have an impact on learning outcomes. The task for the teacher is to find ways of helping children transform their own beliefs into ideas and explanations more consonant with the explanations accepted by conventional science.

Children being taught about living things could be given information directly (for example, 'all these things are living . . . ; these others are not . . .'). The extent to which children have received this information could readily be checked during a question and answer session. However, adoption of this kind of approach to instruction makes little

Age 6 years

"I think they are alive because they move."

Fig. 1. Children's ideas about living things

26

contact with the ideas children bring with them to science and consequently is unlikely to result in the development of new understandings about, in this case, the criteria for judging whether things are living. Such development requires more than simply improving recall of knowledge. It involves the transformation of meaning and can help children to apply their knowledge to new contexts. Rather than adding new examples of living things to their existing list (which might still include inanimate objects), children might be encouraged to consider the nature of living things. For instance, rather than focusing on a single process, such as 'movement', which might have led them to be over-inclusive in their categorisation of living things (water, clockwork toys and the sun all move – see Figure 1) they might begin to think in terms of a combination of life processes (respiration, nutrition, etc). Shifts in understanding of this kind, which contrast with simple recall, involve conceptual change.

STRATEGIES – PROMOTING CONCEPTUAL CHANGE

Finding out children's ideas

The task for the teacher delivering the science curriculum, using a constructivist framework, is first to find out the ideas children hold about the area of science which is being studied. Evidence of children's ideas will form the starting point for the development of subsequent learning activities.

The tendency in the research community has been to find out children's ideas through individual interview. This strategy is not easily undertaken in the primary classroom, where the teacher is charged with finding out the ideas of a large number of children. An alternative approach was adopted by the Science Process and Concepts Exploration (SPACE) Project conducted by researchers at the Centre for Research in Primary Science and Technology at the University of Liverpool and King's College, London. The SPACE project sought to develop classroom-viable techniques for eliciting children's ideas.

An important aspect of eliciting children's ideas is the creation of a classroom environment in which children feel that their ideas are valued. This can be achieved in several ways:

1. Open questions

Open questions which probe children's understanding but, at the same time, convey to the children an interest and regard for their ideas are useful in this respect. Questions have a range of functions in the primary classroom. Often they are 'closed' and used to ascertain

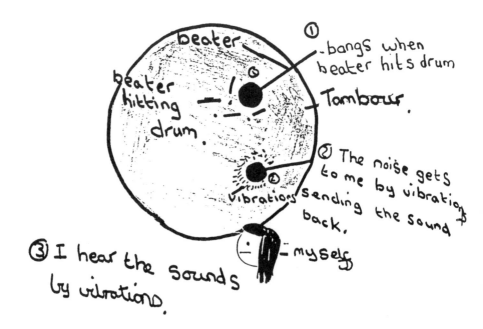

beater

① -bangs when beater hits drum

beater hitting drum.

Tombour.

② The noise gets to me by vibration sending the sound ↗ back.

④ vibrations

-myself

③ I hear the sounds by vibrations.

Age 10 years

Fig. 2. Children's ideas about the production and transmission of sound

whether a particular piece of knowledge has been successfully received. In contrast, questions which include phrases such as 'What do *you* think . . . ?' communicate to children that there is no single appropriate response for which the teacher is searching but rather that all ideas will be valued.

Typically, competing demands on the teacher limit the time available to engage in individual discussions between the child and teacher. However, the teacher is able to plan class discussions in which children can be encouraged through carefully formulated open questions to express their ideas. Teachers engaged in the SPACE research project reported that the successful elicitation of ideas during these discussions required important changes to their practice. One of the most effective means of promoting the expression of ideas is to listen to the emerging ideas. Teachers found, for example, that they needed to wait longer than was their usual practice, for children to respond to questions.

Further encouragement for the expression of ideas can be provided by responding positively to the emerging ideas. Non-verbal cues such as a smile or phrases such as 'That's an interesting idea' convey that, provisionally at least, all ideas are valued. For teachers the adoption of this kind of approach presented new challenges. The acceptance of all ideas was contrary to a more usual practice of providing immediate feedback, either by confirmation or correction of a child's response. Children were also challenged: they became aware that the teacher had moved away from using questions which tended to be searching for a specific response, towards an approach which was overtly interested in the children's own ideas.

2. Drawings

Drawings provide another way in which children can represent their ideas. Pictorial representations can help children to reveal their understanding of abstract or hidden phenomena which might be unavailable in words. During a topic on sound, for instance, children's drawings of how a drum makes a sound revealed an understanding of the production and transmission of sounds (see Figure 2).

Drawings offer other advantages in a busy classroom. They help the teacher to assess the emerging ideas of a whole class or group of children. Furthermore, because they make little demand on writing skills, the teacher is able to move around the classroom, and engage children more freely in discussion than would be the case if the children had to concentrate upon the prolonged process of writing.

An extension of the drawing task is to encourage children to annotate their own drawings and as a further variation to ask children to make sequenced drawings. These can be used to probe children's understanding of changes which occur over time. For instance, to explore children's understanding of growth and development, they might be encouraged to predict how a plant will change over a year; or children might be asked to describe the apparent movement of the sun during the day. Drawings which are supplemented by the teacher or by the child's annotations can offer a means of obtaining a more comprehensive assessment of children's understanding. This can be used as a basis for subsequent learning activities and, in addition, can be used as part of the summative judgements of a child's progress in understanding in science.

Supporting children's developing understanding

One way of addressing teaching and learning in science, once children's ideas have been elicited, would be to focus on direct transmission of science knowledge by the teacher to the children. This strategy would assume that there is a direct correspondence between that which is delivered by the teacher and that which is received by the child. Such a strategy would neglect not only the range of ideas within a class but would also fail to take account of the constructivist view of how children make progress in their own understanding. This strategy would imply that the child is a passive recipient of information. Clearly this would be inconsistent with a view that new knowledge is actively constructed by the learner.

The task for the teacher is to devise an approach to learning which is in harmony with the view that the learner is actively involved in the learning process. In this approach the teacher has to decide how to respond to the range of ideas, once they are elicited. Teachers in the SPACE project developed a number of teaching strategies which, they believed, would effectively support children's learning. The strategies can be classified into four broad groups:

- helping children test their ideas through investigation;

- encouraging generalisations of instances of the concept from one context to another;

- extending the range of evidence available;

- exploring children's use of vocabulary through discussion.

Consideration of the detail of these strategies provides an insight into the development of a teaching repertoire which promotes children's learning in science.

Children learning through investigations

Children can be encouraged to test or explore their ideas by carrying out practical investigations. The process of investigation can provide them with evidence upon which to base a further question, or a conclusion. It is this evidence which is important in persuading children that their existing ideas and explanations might be suspect or incomplete. Such investigations must be carried out scientifically in order that observations, outcomes and conclusions are valid as challenges to or reinforcements of children's ideas.

Investigations which are derived from children's own ideas will, for them, have a purpose. It is likely, then, that the fairness of the investigation can be reinforced by the teacher, encouraging children to identify appropriate variables to control or measure. For example, children investigated their ideas about hearing. They identified a number of variables which they thought were likely to affect their hearing of a sound source:

- distance between source and hearer;

- sound insulation at source or ear;

- use of hearing aid (eg an ear trumpet).

The children recognised that consistency, as regards the volume and pitch of the sound, would be important for a controlled test. They discovered that the further away from a sound source they stood, the fainter was the sound. They also discovered that some people could hear the same sound at a greater distance than others. This led to the suggestion that distance is not the only factor affecting how we hear, and that background noise is significant (Watt and Russell, 1990).

As children develop their ideas about sounds, investigations can be designed to explore the ideas that sounds are produced when something is moving or vibrating and that sound vibrations travel through different materials.

Encouraging generalisations of instances of the concept in different contexts

Children can be helped to develop their understanding of a concept by being provided with opportunities to make comparisons of that concept in two or more contexts. For example, a tank of water provided a context for elicitation of children's ideas about what is happening when water 'disappears'. Children suggested a range of ideas, including a belief that water was disappearing down the legs of the tank (see Figure 3). The teacher introduced other instances of evaporation for the children's consideration, such as towels which dry following a swimming lesson and a wet handprint evaporating from the chalkboard.

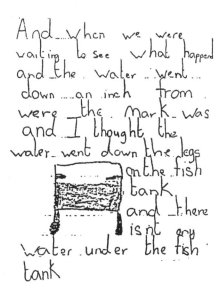

Age 6 years

"And when we were waiting to see what happened and water went down an inch from where the mark was and I thought the water went down the legs on the fish tank and there isn't any water under the fish tank."

Fig. 3. Children's ideas about evaporation (Russell and Watt, 1990)

Children were asked to consider similarities between the different events. Later, they were asked to generate and discuss their own examples of evaporation. Many such events were identified as taking place within the classroom: paper towels dry out in the wastepaper basket; tea or coffee dries in a cup; paint dries in the pots and on the brushes. These examples were designed to invite children to consider the possibility that the process of evaporation occurs when other materials, besides water, are involved.

Extending the range of evidence available

Some ideas in science are not readily accessible in the classroom, because they involve either changes which happen over a long period

32

of time or things which are too small to be visually accessible or which involve great distances. Teachers involved in the SPACE project used secondary sources, such as books, television and video, to help children to develop their ideas. Their use of such media confronted or extended children's initial ideas. In some classrooms, children were encouraged to use books to find evidence for their own ideas or to answer questions which they themselves raised. Video materials, including time-lapse photography, gave children access to events such as the growth and reproduction of plants. Attempts were made by some teachers to make events which were visually imperceptible, perceptible using other senses. For instance, children were encouraged to make links between being able to detect throughout the classroom the smell of perfume from a bottle, using their sense of smell, with the existence of water in the air despite its 'disappearance' from a tank of water (Russell and Watt, 1990).

Exploring vocabulary

Some words have different meanings attached to them in their everyday usage from that which is conventional in science. For instance, for the purposes of science, the classification of those living

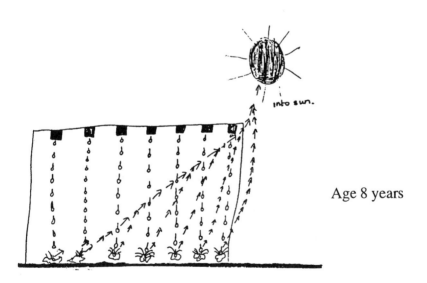

Age 8 years

Fig. 4. Children's ideas about evaporation (Russell and Watt, 1990)

things which are 'animals' includes humans, but in everyday usage, 'animals' often implies 'mammals other than humans'. Many people regard ants as 'insects' but not as 'animals', as would be the case in scientific language. The everyday use of the label 'animal' is thus much more restricted than its use in science.

Children's understanding of 'solid' tends to be restricted to rigid, heavy items. Encouraging them to observe and explore materials such as finely granulated solids and soft solids can help to extend their view of how a solid is defined.

Science learning involves an increasing understanding of technical words such as 'vibration' or 'evaporation' as well as introducing labels such as 'stamen' and 'root'. Children might hold different understandings of the technical words they are using. For instance, 'evaporation' was found to be considered by some children to involve water being 'sucked up' by the sun (see Figure 4).

Opportunities to probe and address children's understanding of the words they use during discussion, or as they carry out investigations, is an important aspect of promoting change in conceptual understanding.

Discussions help children to elaborate and clarify their own ideas. Such interactions provide an opportunity for the teacher to introduce alternative ideas: either conventional scientific explanations or ideas offered by other children. These competing ideas can then become the focus for reflection. It is during such discussions that new ideas are assembled and that developing ideas become more clearly formulated. The interactive nature of the teaching strategies described in this chapter is an important feature of effective teaching and learning in science. It is during these interactions that knowledge is constructed, that children develop an understanding of science and that teachers develop an understanding of the progress children are making.

EVALUATION

Effective implementation of a constructivist approach to teaching requires that teachers have in mind the direction that children's learning might take, as their ideas develop, and at what stage it is appropriate to leave children with the ideas they have. Clearly, teachers need an understanding of the science and a repertoire of appropriate teaching activities.

The National Curriculum in science describes a Programme of Study but does not suggest a sequence for the learning. Research, however, has helped to describe such sequences of learning and some curriculum materials offer support for teachers in terms of describing repertoires of teaching strategies and providing background science knowledge (for example, *Nuffield Primary Science Series*, Black et al 1993).

Strategies for managing open questioning and discussion with children and for planning the investigation of ideas require a willingness to modify curriculum objectives in response to children's emerging ideas. Teachers involved in the SPACE project described some of the benefits, in terms of both an increased confidence in establishing starting points and a better understanding of the direction of children's learning:

> I used to spend too much time talking *at* children not knowing what ideas they already held.

> Now I'll 'have a go'. I feel a lot clearer in my mind where I'm going and why I'm doing things.

(Class teachers)

BIBLIOGRAPHY

Harlen, W. (1993) *Teaching and Learning in Primary Science*. London: Paul Chapman Publishing.

Pfundt, H. and Duit, R. (1994) *Bibliography of Students' Alternative Frameworks and Science Education*. 4th Edition, Institute for Science Education, University of Kiel, IPN.

Piaget, J. (1970) *Genetic Epistemology*. Columbia University Press.

Russell, T. and Watt, D. (1990) *Evaporation and Condensation – Primary SPACE Project Research Report*. Liverpool University Press.

Russell, T., Longden, K. and McGuigan, L. (1991) *Materials – Primary SPACE Project Research Report*. Liverpool University Press.

Russell et al (forthcoming) *Variety of Life – Primary SPACE Project Research Report*. Liverpool University Press.

Vygotsky, L. S. (1978) *Mind in Society: The Development of Higher Psychological Processes*. Harvard University Press.

Watt, D. and Russell, T. (1990) *Sound – Primary SPACE Project Research Report*. Liverpool University Press.

Primary SPACE Project curriculum materials were published in 1993 by Collins Educational under the series title *Nuffield Primary Science*. Black, P. and Harlen, W. (Directors), Russell, T. (Deputy Director), Austin, R., Bell, D., Hughes, A., Longden, K., Meadows, J., McGuigan, L., Osborne, J., Wadsworth, P. and Watt, D.

Earth in Space	*Using Energy*
Electricity and Magnetism	*Variety of Life*
Forces and Movement	*KS2 Teachers' Guide*
Light	*KS1 Teachers' Guide*
Living Processes	*Teachers' Handbook*
Living Things in Their Environment	*In-Service Pack*
Materials	*KS2 Pupils' books (22 titles)*
Rocks, Soil and Weather	*KS1 Pupils' books (11 titles)*
Sound and Music	

3
Language and Learning in Science

David Heywood

INTRODUCTION

Our experience in the world forms the basis from which we speculate about new phenomena. For example, a child who has played with numerous toys which float in water may be expecting a lump of plasticine to float likewise. However, in the case of plasticine, a heavy substance, floating will only take place if it is shaped in a particular way. The child might seek to fit this new experience within its existing framework of understanding and in this, thinking is developed. There is a constant juxtaposition between that which we know (the concrete) and our new experiences (or abstraction) in making sense of ideas. This experience may be enhanced through language between the teacher and the child.

Because science is often in conflict with our common-sense way of looking at the world, it sometimes doesn't make sense (Wolpert, 1992). The problem for the teacher is that explanations for phenomena and the concepts being developed derive from a vocabulary rooted in everyday experience. It is from this vocabulary that we reason about scientific ideas. In science, words and phrases are used precisely to avoid confusion and ambiguity. For example, when added to warm tea, sugar goes into solution, the sugar is the solute and the warm tea the solvent. Here we have a familiar phenomenon described precisely with an unfamiliar vocabulary. For the learner, scientific ideas must develop or 'evolve', demanding interpretation in such a way that some words take on a different meaning.

In order to understand and make sense of scientific ideas, we need to relate them to our existing experience which is framed in the language in which we reason and make sense of the world. In this chapter I wish to explore the idea that the conceptual struggle we encounter when redefining words to interpret scientific meaning is an integral element of the scientific enterprise. This struggle, although a problem, is a necessary step in the process of scientific learning.

The acquisition of vocabulary in which we develop a common-sense view of the world is a prerequisite for the development of scientific ideas. The process of developing scientific reasoning involves more than the acquisition of new words into existing vocabulary, important though this is. The central issue is one of interpretation which can involve either the redefining of words in our existing vocabulary, sometimes in a radically different way, or the incorporation of new words.

Language is central to the structure of reasoning. In learning science we acquire words with specific definitions and translate these definitions into our vocabulary, often without being given sufficient opportunity to explore the ideas underpinned by the words. For example, I may acquire the word 'acceleration' and translate the scientific definition that it means a change of speed with respect to time into my existing vocabulary without constructing a scientific understanding of the concept. This is common in many people's non-scientific ideas concerning such phenomena as falling objects where acceleration is not qualitatively distinguished from velocity. In order to construct further meaning and develop qualitative understanding associated with the words, a further stage in the process is required, that of interpretation.

In making sense of ideas in science, the learner is involved in an evolutionary process requiring the constant refinement, redefinition and interpretation of meaning of words. The evolution of ideas is therefore a core element of teaching and learning in science at all levels and should be actively encouraged in the development of understanding. It requires the interpretation of new situations with respect to our existing world experience.

A LANGUAGE FRAMEWORK FOR LEARNING IN SCIENCE

It is useful to devise a language framework which offers some insight into the mechanisms experienced when confronted with difficult ideas in science.

1. **Acquisition of vocabulary.** This is the first stage of the process. Words are acquired through discourse in social interaction and are given meaning from the experiences we associate with them. For example, the word 'weight' acquires meaning through experience of the particular property of an object which is different from its other properties such as shape, colour or size.

2. **Translation.** The second part of the process is one of translation. This is context related. The word 'weight' acquires further meaning through association with heavy and light. The meaning of the word is translated into understanding through comparison and contrast. Weight is, however, commonly associated with size and the distinction between weight and size often requires refinement and reinforcement in different contexts. This process of translation from a range of everyday common-sense experiences, although important, is insufficient in itself in developing a scientific understanding of the world.

3. **Interpretation.** Many scientific terms such as weight can be interpreted in different ways. There is the everyday meaning, which is a sense of heaviness, frequently associated with bulk, and there is the scientific meaning which is that weight is a force. If understanding of the word is to evolve from the everyday to the scientific then it is necessary to provide experiences that draw attention to the new or extended meaning of the word. As with translation, the opportunity to compare and contrast is integral to the process. This might be achieved, for example, by drawing attention to the effect that the force of weight has on structures or floating objects.

Two important aspects of this process need to be considered. First, the categories in the framework are not discrete. They are simply meant to offer some insight into the process experienced when new ideas are confronted which require interpretation of the world using words in a different context or with different meaning from their everyday use. Recognising such processes in our own learning raises our awareness as teachers of the language difficulties encountered when children are confronted with ideas in science which do not fit with their view of the world. Second, the interpretative process is never complete. It requires the constant review of words and their meaning in different contexts. Each stage of the process involves comparison and contrast of the new with existing experience in order for ideas to evolve. The evolution of ideas is common to both the teacher and the learner.

STRATEGIES FOR LANGUAGE DEVELOPMENT IN SCIENCE

What does this mean for the teaching and learning of science in primary education? The following examples illustrate aspects of this process in three conceptual areas, spin and rotation, weight and forces and electricity. Each makes a unique specific learning demand on the individual requiring a review (on occasions radical) of existing use of words in order to reinterpret their meaning as understanding evolves. The conceptual areas are illustrative of the language framework outlined and the teaching implications are identified in each case. The process is common to all learners of science and for this reason the examples are not restricted to children's learning.

CHALLENGES IN THE LANGUAGE PROCESS

Spin and rotation

Towards interpretation: a conceptual journey
Traditionally primary schools have always developed awareness in children of the passage of time through work on the seasons and parts of the day. Telling the time and the idea of chronology is a basic skill and we build an understanding of time through our observations of the passage of time and the experiences we associate with it. The predictable repeatability of the seasons and night and day help us to organise our lives and make sense of the world around us. Their cyclical nature not only affects our physiological state but is also embedded in our cultural and spiritual world. Working in this area of the science curriculum requires the development of understanding.

What level of understanding is therefore necessary and what are the difficulties the learner is likely to encounter? It is quite acceptable for a three-year-old to explain darkness as a consequence of the sun going to sleep. A similar explanation given by the same child at eleven would be inadequate.

The key ideas that the learner encounters in this area include scale (of both time and distance), the relative movement of objects in space and the knowledge of cycles being repeatable. There is also the problem of two-dimensional representation of three-dimensional objects in space.

It is well within the capacity of primary children at Key Stage 2 (7–11 years) to understand that we have night and day because the earth spins on its own axis once every twenty-four hours turning away from and then facing the sun to give night and day. This is regularly repeatable and within their experience. If, however, the question of changing daylight length throughout the year is raised then this requires a consideration of both spin and orbit, a complex problem which often requires reinterpretation of the word 'spin'. As an example of the difficulty of holding one concept (spin) with respect to another (orbit) I shall refer to work on these ideas with primary teachers.

Most people have direct experience of spin and hence have an internalised interpretation of what the word means gained from everyday experiences in which the word is used, such as a spinning top or a fairground ride or even the feeling of being intoxicated! The idea is directly challenged when we refer to the rate of the moon's spin about its own axis. This creates a problem in understanding why we only see one face of the moon from earth.

> The reason that you see only one side of the moon from earth is because its rate of spin is the same as its rate of orbit.

This precise way of expressing a complex idea is intended to reduce the possibility of ambiguity but in fact does not necessarily create understanding because there is likely to be a language difficulty. In such statements learners often need some time to decipher the actual words and the way the words are organised in relation to each other. This phenomenon of spin in heavenly bodies creates a considerable degree of conflict and most learners find difficulty in resolving the fact and making it fit with their current concept of spin because spinning is usually associated with relatively rapid movement as in the examples of the spinning top and the fairground ride. This would be an example of what I have termed translation, the working out of what the actual sentence is saying. The process of translation, although not necessarily synonymous with understanding, is an important element in the learner recognising a lack of coherence in their existing notion of spin 'fitting' with the statement.

Understanding evolves from this recognition that there is a problem with the use of the word 'spin'. Firstly, there is the dimension of working from the everyday use of the word (spinning on the spot) to

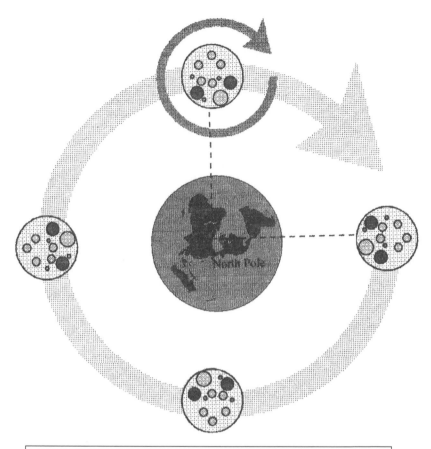

As the Moon travels through a quarter of its orbit, it must spin through 90º on its own axis in order to keep the same side facing Earth. It spins at the same rate as its orbits – threrefore only the one side is visible from Earth whether Earth is spinning or not!

Fig. 5. The moon's orbit of the Earth looking from above the North Pole

an unfamiliar use of the word (spinning while orbiting). Secondly, the word 'spin' takes its meaning not only from previous experience but also from its relationship to other words around it. The significance of this is illustrated in the interrelationship of the words 'spin' and 'orbit' in the statement given. The statement demands a consideration of one with respect to the other. Only when a relationship between the two is recognised can the explanation have coherence. In the case in point, the spin needs to be at the same rate as the orbit for the observable facts to fit (see Figure 5).

42

This requires the ideas to be considered simultaneously, a task much more difficult than considering each separately. What is required conceptually is a reinterpretation of meaning of existing vocabulary, 'spin' and 'orbit'.

It is important that the teacher is aware that this process of reinterpretation is integral to science learning and that it involves more than simply acquiring words with a specific meaning into the vocabulary. Even when words exist within our vocabulary and have been translated with respect to existing experience, their meaning needs to be constantly examined in different contexts. This affords opportunity for reinterpretation. Although children in the primary school are no longer required to understand the phases of the moon, the process is recognisably similar to that of developing children's understanding of the cause of the seasons which also requires them to consider both spin and orbit in relation to each other, albeit at a less sophisticated level. This process of interpretation and refinement enables the construction of increasingly sophisticated concepts to take place. Often the interpretation of words is redefined in terms of other words.

The second example illustrates the point where an interpretation of the word 'density' evolves from a consideration of the concept that weight is a force and that an object's weight for size determines whether it floats or sinks in water.

Weight and forces

Floating and 'thinking'

In English we often use the same words to mean different things. We also use different words for the same thing. For example, when investigating floating and sinking we may use the word 'weight' when we mean mass and interchange the word 'size' for volume. It is no surprise that when asked to explain the behaviour of objects in water, young children usually focus initially on the object's property of weight, that is, heavy objects sink and light objects float. Simple practical trial and error should reveal this not to be the case and it is not too difficult for learners to perceive that it is not just the object's property of weight that determines its behaviour in water, because some light objects sink and some heavy objects float. If this is pursued further an important link can be made between an object's weight and its size and its behaviour in water. We call this relationship between weight and size 'density'. In common vocabulary the word 'density' can have a quite different meaning from that which would be attributed to it in science. Equally, the common everyday use of the word 'weight' is unlikely to be associated with the idea of weight as a force being dependent on gravity. To speak of a person losing weight might include a change of shape by redistributing mass to fit with the body fashion of the time and for most people, weight change does manifest itself in an individual changing shape. This can lead to the implicit notion that smaller equals lighter. From such experiences our perceptions and interpretations evolve.

The relationship between weight and size is not nearly as straightforward as it might first appear to be. This is well documented in Piaget's (1971) classical research on children's conservation of weight and volume. It is not just children who struggle with this. Take a common activity in floating and sinking: that of making a ball of plasticine into a different shape such that it will float. Then ask, what is it about the object that has been changed and what property of the object has remained unaltered. Adults will recognise that its weight has been conserved and that the volume of the object has increased. That is, the object has become light for its size and therefore floats. The idea of a relationship between weight and size is a qualitative beginning of understanding of density and how this is related to floating and sinking. Despite this, difficulties still remain for many people with respect to what it is that has changed density, the object or the material from which the object is made. It is not uncommon to find learners taking a smaller ball of plasticine in anticipation that something so light will float, clearly demonstrating the confusion that exists in some children's minds when considering weight and size. Having been through the learning process and having direct tactile experience of the forces involved when objects are immersed in water, the word 'density' can now be defined in real terms (weight for size), which could look something like this:

> We have a word which describes whether an object is heavy or light for its size, the word is density. Density is weight for size.

This is a way of quantifying what we have qualitatively explored, namely, that objects which are heavy for their size exert a downward force which is greater than the upthrust of the water, and so they sink. Conversely, the upthrust of water on objects which are light for their size balances the downward force of the object and the object floats (see Figure 6).

This assimilation of ideas has required a reinterpretation of the

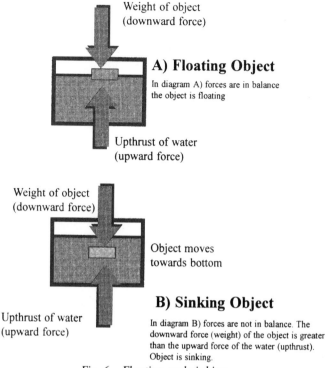

Weight of object
(downward force)

A) Floating Object

In diagram A) forces are in balance
the object is floating

Upthrust of water
(upward force)

Weight of object
(downward force)

Object moves
towards bottom

B) Sinking Object

Upthrust of water
(upward force)

In diagram B) forces are not in balance. The
downward force (weight) of the object is greater
than the upward force of the water (upthrust).
Object is sinking.

Fig. 6. Floating and sinking

words 'weight' and 'size' and the introduction of a new word 'density' to describe the relationship between the two in terms of an object's properties. The definition of weight is, however, conceptualised in a fundamentally different way from the everyday use of the word. To interpret rather than just translate the word 'density', the idea that weight is a force and the property of a fluid exerting an opposing force on an immersed object need to be explored to build a qualitative understanding of the concept to which the word relates. Of course, there is always a catch: physicists would require the use of the word 'mass' instead of 'weight' and 'size' would need to be replaced with the specific mathematical concept of 'volume' – yet another example of the process of acquisition, translation and interpretation in action.

The final example is illustrative of how words in a new context derive from our existing use of them but evolve to take on new meaning in the process of interpretation demanded when working from the concrete to abstraction.

Electricity

From the known to the unknown – analogical reasoning and the abstract

It is one thing to define and refine, quite another to journey from the known to the unknown in terms of reasoning about a phenomenon with which you can have little if any direct experience. Nowhere is this difficulty more pronounced than in the study of electricity where the electricity itself is intangible and the only first-hand experience encountered involves manifestations of electricity, such as a bulb lighting. To overcome this problem it is common to offer explanation through analogy.

Analogical reasoning is based on the idea of comparison with and contrast to existing experience. For it to be successful, the analogy must resonate with the learner's existing understanding and provide a reference point and foundation to which the learner can relate. The words used in the analogy must therefore derive from a vocabulary which has meaning and has been assimilated into everyday language. An example would be the use of the word 'current' which from common experience would probably be related to the flow of water. A water analogy is indeed quite common in the teaching of electricity to explore ideas associated with the relationship between the flow of current and resistance in electric circuits. Whatever the analogy being used, the process is the same. The purpose is to enhance understanding of the unknown through constant reference to the known so that eventually words are reinterpreted to take on new meaning in different contexts. This is another example of comparison and contrast.

A perennial problem with this process is the fact that under increasingly sophisticated scrutiny all analogies break down (Driver, 1983) and the learner's demand for explanation, that something concrete to which they can refer in order to understand the behaviour under investigation, is no longer satisfied by the analogy. There is a positive way of looking at this problem. Wrestling with ideas is part of the scientific endeavour in attempting to make a coherent story of the world around us. Admittedly the stories become ever more sophisticated but for each individual the story will be interpreted differently. This is why some analogies suit some learners more than others. The meaning the words have in new contexts are determined by their relationship to each other and the visual images created are dependent on the application of the idea. So to think of current in a circuit it is necessary to draw on the visual imagery which the word 'current' evokes.

The flow of electricity is, however, not exactly like the flow of water and it is therefore necessary to conceptualise the phenomenon in a slightly different way and to build and adjust the comparison through identifying the differences as well as the similarities. In so doing a new picture is visualised. This can only be achieved if the concept under consideration relates tangibly to existing understanding. Interpretation evolves from consolidated experience to abstract meaning.

EVALUATING THE LANGUAGE PROCESS

We need to recognise that when a learner is confronted with scientific ideas their common-sense view will influence their perceptions. We often use words from everyday experiences in a quite different way from the way in which words are used in science. In making sense of ideas in science, therefore, it is often necessary to interpret words in our existing vocabulary differently. This is an evolutionary process in which we constantly develop from our 'concrete' everyday experience and build an understand of the new meaning. In this interpretative process our ideas are challenged and developed and the abstract itself takes on meaning and becomes more accessible.

Practical experience is an important element in this process and can be useful in exploring and testing ideas, as, for example, in feeling the force of upthrust on an object in water and its effect on the weight of an immersed object. In terms of the framework described such an activity would provide opportunity for language acquisition. For very young children the words 'floating' and 'sinking' may need exploration, while older children can be introduced to such words as 'upthrust' and 'displacement'. It takes time for the words to take on different meanings and it is common in such processes for the learner constantly to refer the scientific ideas to common everyday use of words.

This is part of the translation process in which the learner attempts to make sense of how the vocabulary is used in a specific context. It is therefore understandable that a learner often holds two apparently contradictory views, the common-sense one and the scientific one (Solomon, 1992). However, practical activity is in itself insufficient in developing scientific meaning.

For example, the idea that it is an object's weight for size which determines whether it floats or sinks does not necessarily develop from direct tactile experience as described in the above activity. This concept will not just evolve without teacher intervention and support.

It is therefore essential that the teacher identifies the key ideas to be developed in such an activity and is alert to how such ideas manifest themselves when children try to make sense of why some heavy objects float. Children may observe that heavy objects which float are big and this may lead to the recognition that it is necessary to consider not just the weight of the object but how big it is as well. Such reasoning involves interpretation. In this particular instance teacher and learner would be preparing the foundation on which to develop the idea of weight for size, a prerequisite for the concept of density.

The task of the science teacher, therefore, is not just to find ways of constructing the scientifically accepted meaning of words such that definitions are acceptable; rather, the teacher should focus on the exploration of ideas through relating concepts to existing experience using language which is familiar to the learner. Recognition of this would result in a more positive approach to the teaching and learning of science.

BIBLIOGRAPHY

Driver, R. (1983) *The Pupil as Scientist*. Milton Keynes: Open University Press.
Piaget, J. (1971) *Understanding Causality*. New York: W. W. Norton & Company Inc.
Solomon, J. (1992) *Getting to Know about Energy – in School and Society*. London: Falmer Press.
Sutton, C. (1992) *Words, Science and Learning*. Buckingham: Open University Press.
Vygotsky, L. S. (1962) *Thought and Language*. Cambridge, Mass.: MIT Press.
Wolpert, W. (1992) *The Unnatural Nature of Science*. London: Faber and Faber.

PART 2

Issues of Quality in Provision

4
Progression in Learning in Science

Stuart Naylor and Brenda Keogh

INTRODUCTION: WHAT IS PROGRESSION IN LEARNING?

When children are confronted by new events or experiences they go through a process of attempting to link these new observations with their existing scientific understanding. They struggle to make sense of new experience in terms of their previous experience and in doing so they must attempt to modify the concepts which they hold. This is when learning occurs.

When the children's conceptual development becomes more complex, more coherent and more scientific then progression is evident. However, progression may not always be so clear cut. Sometimes there may be little apparent change in their ideas, but they are accumulating experience, strengthening their understanding and extending the range of situations in which their newly forming ideas apply. This process of consolidation also indicates progression.

Sometimes progression may be indicated by children appearing to regress in their understanding. This can happen when they set aside their initial ideas in order to build a more complete understanding of a concept. During the process of reorganisation of their ideas they may appear to be confused, but this can still be an important stage in progression in their understanding.

The recent changes in the National Curriculum for science indicate how progression should be viewed. Progression is more than simply tackling additional content areas of science. The level descriptions for science describe different levels of understanding of science concepts,

51

where the same experience may be understood at different levels of complexity by different children. Progression is concerned with progress through these levels of understanding, not with any particular sequence of concepts.

Hence, progression can be viewed as the process by which children develop their ideas or skills. It can refer to small steps in learning which happen quickly as well as to more complex developments in learning which may take many years. It has reference to what children have achieved already and to where they should be going in their learning. Progression is about something that happens to learners, not about the way that the curriculum is structured.

There are important links between progression and differentiation. Although they describe different processes there is considerable overlap in their implications for teachers. In planning for progression teachers will attempt to take the children's current level of development into account. Since the children frequently will be at different stages in their development, planning for progression will require the teacher to consider the need for providing differentiated learning experiences. The outcome of these experiences should be progression in the children's learning.

CHALLENGES

Achieving progression in learning

Finding out the children's ideas
Research, such as that carried out by the SPACE Project (1990–93), shows us the importance of taking the children's ideas into account when planning for teaching. The reason is that the children's existing ideas make a difference to how they perceive new ideas. In other words, what they think now will affect their future learning. Therefore in order to build on the children's ideas the teacher must have access to those ideas. The challenge for teachers is how to do this without taking away from time which could be spent on supporting their learning.

Responding to children's ideas
The purpose of finding out about the children's ideas is to respond to them in a way that challenges their ideas and promotes further development (progression) in their learning. Through being aware of their ideas the teacher is able to help the children to test their ideas

in a scientific manner (Harlen, 1993). The Non-Statutory Guidance for Science recognises this and stresses the importance of 'taking the pupil's initial ideas seriously' (NCC, 1989).

The challenge to the teacher is how to respond to all the individual children in a class, especially now that average class sizes are increasing in primary schools. Although it could be relatively straight-forward to find a suitable response for one or two children's ideas, doing this for a whole class is much more challenging. Furthermore, there may be the additional problem presented by the necessity to adhere to a scheme of work and yet still be in a position to respond to differing levels of knowledge and understanding amongst the children.

Helping the children to develop their ideas
Research shows that children's ideas can be surprisingly resistant to change (Osborne and Freyberg, 1985). Providing new experiences and ideas may not be sufficient to convince children that their ideas need to develop further. The challenge is how to help the children to see that they need to modify their ideas when they may feel that their existing ideas are perfectly satisfactory.

Making use of information from assessment and
record-keeping
The recent shift away from assessment and record-keeping systems which recorded each child's progress against individual Statements of Attainment has been welcomed by many teachers. What Dearing (1994) described as 'cumbersome and over complex' recording systems have not been a particularly useful way to plan for progression in learning. Although in the past teachers recorded detailed information about individual children's achievements, much of this information was too complex and therefore of limited value in planning for progression. The challenge for teachers is to decide what to record in order to help plan for progression.

STRATEGIES

Planning for progression in scientific ideas

Finding out about children's developing ideas about science in the world
A view of learning which sees learning as change in concepts or ideas has important implications for teachers. Planning to promote change

in the children's ideas means creating opportunities to take their ideas into account. Many of the traditional approaches to finding out the children's concepts view this as quite separate from developing those concepts or ideas. Finding out the children's ideas may appear to be at the expense of the children's learning. However, there are alternatives to this view.

Some approaches can provide opportunities to find out about the children's ideas through activities which are themselves a stimulus to learning. These dual-purpose activities will usually involve children in thinking about their ideas, discussing their ideas with each other and having an obvious purpose for sharing their ideas. Suitable approaches include concept maps (White and Gunstone, 1992), annotated drawings, sorting and classifying and using concept cartoons (Keogh and Naylor, 1996). The Teachers' Guides in the Nuffield Primary Science (1993) scheme include many examples of worthwhile activities designed to find out about the children's ideas, where the activities can also support their learning. These kinds of activities help to draw together teaching, learning and assessment and promote better progression in learning.

Helping children to develop their ideas

One way of anticipating the children's possible starting points comes from recent research. There is an extensive literature which describes the kinds of ideas that children are likely to hold at different ages. The Teachers' Guides for Nuffield Primary Science (1993), SPACE Project reports (1990–93) and Driver et al (1994) are all excellent sources of information about children's ideas. The research findings are particularly helpful for identifying the likely areas of confusion or misunderstanding which may arise. Teachers will find that being able to anticipate many of the ideas that children hold will be helpful in planning to develop their ideas.

The problem of how to take the individual children's ideas into account when class sizes are large is a major challenge for teachers. One possibility sometimes suggested is to group the children according to their ideas. However, this approach requires precision in judging what is the present state of knowledge of all the children in the class. In small schools it is unlikely to be feasible to consider this at all.

Perhaps a more realistic approach would be to offer some degree of choice within activities so that the children can make their own judgement about how best to test their ideas. Even though their ideas may be very different, they can often be tested by broadly similar activities. In other words, finding out and using the children's ideas does not normally require completely different activities for each child (Nuffield, 1996). An example of this would be seen when children are investigating the factors which affect how quickly an object falls. Although the children may have different ideas about which factors are important (eg weight, size, colour, shape) they would investigate their ideas using the same kinds of tests. The teacher's role would be to help them to explore possibilities for investigation and to make connections between their investigations and their existing ideas.

Practical activities on their own will not guarantee that children will modify and restructure their ideas (Keogh and Naylor, 1993). For this to be successful the experience is likely to require:

- active involvement, so that the children's own ideas play an important role;

- a clear sense of purpose which is clear to the children, not just to the teacher;

- sharing ideas in groups throughout the activity, so that individual children have the opportunity to clarify and rethink their ideas;

- opportunity for the children to test a range of ideas, so that they can see that some ideas are more successful at explaining their experience than others;

- helping children to make connections between any new experience and their existing ideas.

The Nuffield Primary Science Teachers' Guides (1993) provide extensive examples of activities which offer these kinds of opportunities. Presenting alternative views through concept cartoons can be a particularly effective way to help the children to reflect on and develop their ideas (Keogh and Naylor, 1996). Children can also help each other to develop their understanding through sharing their ideas, identifying alternative viewpoints, considering what evidence is available and devising suitable investigations. Having a variety of viewpoints within each group makes this kind of productive discussion more likely.

Making record-keeping useful

What is it that teachers need to know in order to plan for progression? Some knowledge of the children's previous experience is necessary for making long- and medium-term plans for a class. This can be provided quite simply by keeping annotated plans for each topic which will indicate the range of experiences which most of the children will have had. To be effective this must be a whole-school responsibility rather than something which is left to individual teachers.

What about planning for progression for individual children? Very detailed records for each child quickly become repetitive and are difficult to use in practice. The simplest form of record is one which notes exceptional rather than typical progress. The teacher can then assume that a child has made typical progress unless there is some statement to the contrary. Records such as these will be easy to use and will make planning for progression more realistic.

In either case, making use of records of children's progress involves seeing these records as provisional, since it is difficult to anticipate in any detail how children will respond to any particular activity or experience. There is never any guarantee that records will provide an accurate prediction of what children's ideas are today. However much teachers know about the children's ideas, learning depends on the interaction between the teacher, the children and the activity. Using as wide a range of approaches as possible for probing, challenging and developing the children's ideas will provide the maximum number of opportunities for interactions to be productive and for learning to take place. Offering opportunities for children to contribute their own ideas will also help to ensure that they see activities as relevant and meaningful.

Planning for progression in learning how to work scientifically

Progression in individual skills
Progression in using scientific procedures is about gradually developing from random and unstructured exploration to systematic and focused investigation. The level descriptions for Attainment Target 1 in the National Curriculum for Science provide a useful outline of what this might mean in practice. They provide some sense of how children might develop their abilities in relation to the planning, doing and reviewing phases of scientific activities.

Embedded within the level descriptions for Attainment Target 1 are several separate skills, such as making predictions, selecting and using suitable apparatus, carrying out fair tests and presenting data. It is possible to get some indication of the likely progression in each of these skills from the level descriptions, though other authors offer a more comprehensive view and more detailed guidance.

Goldsworthy and Feasy (1994) describe a number of skills in some detail. For each separate skill they outline how progression might be identified and what teachers can do to enable children to develop further. Their list includes:

- children raising questions;

- predicting and hypothesising;

- fair testing;

- measuring;

- constructing and using tables;

- constructing and using graphs and charts;

- explaining results;

- evaluating investigations.

For example, when children are investigating how the size of a piece of jelly affects how quickly it dissolves, they can predict how long it will take to dissolve. Progress in predicting might be identified according to the following sequence:

- Making a simple prediction: 'I think the little pieces will dissolve first.'

- Making a prediction and trying to give a reason, but not really providing any more information: 'I think the little pieces will dissolve first because they're little.'

- Making a prediction and giving reasons based on everyday experience: 'I think the little pieces will dissolve first because my Dad breaks it into little pieces when he makes jelly.'

- Making a prediction and giving reasons based on knowledge of similar situations: 'I think the little pieces will dissolve first because little bits of sugar dissolve faster than a sugar lump.'

- Making a hypothesis to attempt to explain dissolving: 'I think the little pieces will dissolve first because the water can attack them more easily.'

- Making a hypothesis which shows understanding of scientific concepts involved: 'I think the little pieces will dissolve first because there are more surfaces in touch with the water.'

(*Source*: Goldsworthy and Feasey, 1994)

Nuffield (1996) also offers pointers to identifying progression in these individual skills, noting examples such as expressing ideas in a form which can be investigated, observing carefully, using a range of measuring devices and quantifying their investigations. Each of these skills can be learnt. Teachers therefore have an important role in providing opportunities for children to develop these skills and directly teaching these skills when necessary.

The children's own awareness of how to work scientifically is also an aspect of progression. As they become more aware of what being scientific means they will be able to use a scientific approach more effectively. Teachers can support the development of this awareness by encouraging children to reflect on the approach that they have used, rather than simply reviewing how their ideas have developed at the end of an investigation.

Progression in developing each of these individual skills is important, but this is only part of the picture. In order to be useful these separate skills need to be combined in a coherent way. The whole purpose of developing the individual skills is to be able to use them to make sense of new experiences and to test ideas. Opportunities therefore will need to be provided for children (particularly the older children) to work through the whole process of a scientific investigation reasonably independently on some occasions.

Linking progression in scientific ideas and scientific skills

When it comes to planning for progression in scientific ideas little detailed guidance is available for teachers. Authors such as Peacock (1991) have provided lists of stages in the development of concepts. Although such lists are valuable they may not be easy to assimilate and they are not readily available to teachers.   .

In previous versions of the National Curriculum the sequence of Statements of Attainment gave some indication of what progression in ideas might be expected, and many teachers found this useful as an aid to planning. The current National Curriculum documentation provides no such guidance. Level descriptions indicate broad levels of understanding, but not in relation to any specified sequence of concepts. The Programmes of Study give an outline of the curriculum, which is helpful for promoting continuity across key stages but provide very little guidance in planning for progression. How activities should be planned to promote different levels of understanding is not spelt out.

Linking progression in understanding with progression in the use of skills can provide some degree of guidance. Harlen (1993, p. 40) notes that 'the development of understanding in science is . . . dependent on the ability to carry out process skills in a scientific manner'. As the children's ideas become more detailed, more complex and more abstract, so the skills that they need to test their ideas also become more complex and sophisticated.

The level descriptions for Attainment Target 1 also point to important links between progression in using scientific procedures and progression in the children's understanding of relevant scientific ideas. This can be seen in the expected shift from simple descriptions of observations to comparisons, then to explanations, and finally to explanations that are related to their scientific knowledge and understanding. This expected pattern of development can be taken into account in planning learning opportunities for children and in deciding on a suitable level of challenge in an activity.

In the framework shown in Figure 7 we have attempted to provide some guidance on how conceptual understanding and skills might be linked. The framework gives a broad indication of how different levels of scientific skills will be brought to bear when children are attempting to develop their ideas. It shows how, whatever the age of the learner, exploring is likely to precede investigating which will precede researching when children are developing a concept. It points to the importance of younger children being encouraged to concentrate on experiencing and exploring phenomena in order to develop their scientific ideas. Older children will normally be encouraged to place more emphasis on systematic investigation and research (though there is still a need for exploration). As their ideas develop the shift from observable to more abstract ideas highlights the limits to what children can 'discover' on their own. As ideas become more complex, access to other sources of information becomes essential.

As children become more confident in their ideas they will be able to investigate their ideas in more challenging and sophisticated ways. By providing a general outline of the typical sequence of development, the framework can give a provisional indication of what type of activity is likely to be suitable for children at various stages in their learning in any area of science. This can help in curriculum planning which promotes progression.

The framework can also be used to decide how any particular activity might be adjusted to make it either more accessible or more demanding. As children engage in an activity the teacher may decide that the level of challenge in the activity needs to be adjusted during the lesson. By providing a general indication of how the level of challenge may vary, the framework can give a provisional indication

General Framework	The Teacher's Role	The Pupil's Role	An Illustration
Ideas emerge as generalisations from experience	Provide opportunities to experience phenomena and talk about them	Something happens – I see what happens or someone helps me to see. I look more closely – have I seen what is really happening?	Ice melts. It feels cold, it feels wet . . . the outside melts first
Exploring further. Thinking and talking, beginning to search for patterns	Provide opportunities to explore ideas further . . . encourage closer observation, thinking and talking and the beginning of searching for patterns	Does it always happen the same? Can I change what happens or can I see something making it change?	Sometimes it melts faster. I can warm it up. I can wrap it up
Asking why – attempting to explain	Helping the pupils to raise questions and search for possible explanations	Why does it happen? Can I explain what I think?	When it was near the radiator it melted faster. When I wrapped it in newspaper it did not melt as fast
Using ideas to guide more systematic investigation	Help pupils to use a more scientific approach to enable them to develop their ideas	What do I think makes a difference? Can I change what happens in a systematic way so that I really find out what matters?	It seems to be something to do with being warmer or stopping it getting warm. I can measure the temperature, the time etc. I can try to identify variables
Further investigation – predicting – testing – applying	Help pupils to confirm and challenge their ideas through hypothesising, predicting, testing and applying, quantifying where necessary	Can I try it in other ways and get the same pattern of results?	I will use bigger blocks of ice/higher temperature/lower temperature/different insulation etc.

Asking questions identifies the need for further information and more abstract ideas:	Provide challenges which help the pupils to see that expectations in observable terms may not be enough	Can I explain what is happening in observable terms?	The higher the temperature – the faster it melts. The greater the volume – the longer it takes to melt. More insulation – slower melting
-from the learner -from some other source	Encourage the search for abstract ideas. Provide access to sources of information	Is there more I can find out or can you tell me to help me to understand more about why it happens?	You tell me about particles. I read a book with information about solids, liquids and gases (I am unlikely to discover atoms on my own)
Acquiring and using more abstract concepts	Provide illustrations and opportunities to apply new abstract ideas	Can I use what I know to explain what is happening in non-observable terms?	I can now explain melting, using what I know about particles and explain why the temperature makes a difference
Systematic inquiry involving hypothesising and testing: describing and testing possible applications	Provide opportunities for more systematic inquiry involving these abstract ideas, including possible applications	Can I use the idea to explain other changes?	I realise that condensation, freezing and evaporation all use the same theory
Building up relationships between abstract concepts	Provide illustration and opportunities to relate their learning to other abstract concepts	Can I use the idea to explain a greater range of events?	I can explain ice floating (volume and density) and think about the possible arrangement of particles

Fig. 7. A framework for sequencing scientific ideas, skills and activities. (Source: Jarman, Keogh and Naylor, 1994)

of how the activity might best be modified. Further details of this framework can be found in Jarman, Keogh and Naylor (1994).

Finding a realistic perspective on progression

Clearly progression in learning is something for teachers to aim for. To what extent they can achieve it is less certain. The National Curriculum makes some attempt to build progression into the curriculum, but whilst this may provide curriculum continuity it cannot guarantee progression in learning (Driver et al, 1994). Attempting to plan for a close match between individual children's learning and their current level of understanding is worthwhile but fraught with difficulty. Dearing (1993) recognised this in stating that 'learning is a messy business'. It is important to keep in mind that the kind of planning, interacting and responding which is possible when working with a group of six children is out of the question with a class of 26 or 36.

As with differentiation (see Chapter 5), regarding plans as provisional, adjusting the activity and learning environment in the light of the children's responses and attempting to share the responsibility for learning with the children are useful and realistic strategies. Although they provide no guarantee that progression in learning will occur, they do help to make it more likely.

EVALUATING PROGRESS IN PROGRESSION

This chapter has attempted to map out some of the challenges involved in promoting progression in learning science and some of the strategies which can be helpful for making progression in learning more likely. These strategies could be used as indicators of progression in learning by an individual teacher or by a school. Which of them are used at the moment? How frequently are they used? Do teachers know which strategies are in use? Could any of them be used more effectively? These issues will be taken up in Book 2, where the emphasis will be on in-service activities for teachers to support reflection on existing practice and extension to it.

Another perspective on evaluating progress in progression in learning comes from considering the children's scientific skills and understanding. What evidence is there that scientific learning is successful for each group of children? What evidence is there that the pace and the nature of their scientific learning is planned and monitored systematically? What evidence is there that learning in any particular topic builds effectively on previous learning? Further guidance on questions such as these is given in Chapter 14, which deals with the whole question of monitoring and evaluation.

BIBLIOGRAPHY

Dearing, R. (1993) *The National Curriculum and its Assessment: An Interim Report*. York: National Curriculum Council.

Dearing, R. (1993) *The National Curriculum and its Assessment*. London: School Curriculum and Assessment Authority.

Driver, R. et al. (1994) *Making Sense of Secondary Science*. London: Routledge.

Goldsworthy, A. and Feasey, R. (1994) *Making Sense of Primary Science Investigations*. Hatfield: Association for Science Education.

Harlen, W. (1993) Children's Learning in Science, in R. Sherrington (ed.) *ASE Primary Science Teachers' Handbook*. Hatfield: Association for Science Education/Simon and Schuster.

Jarman, R. Keogh, B. and Naylor, S. (1994) *I've Done This Before: Continuity and Progression in School Science*. Hatfield: Association for Science Education.

Keogh, B. and Naylor, S. (1993) Learning in science: another way in. *Primary Science Review*, no. 26, pp. 22–23.

Keogh, B. and Naylor, S. (1996) *Scientists and Primary Schools: a Practical Guide*. Sandbach: Millgate House Publishers.

National Curriculum Council (1989) *Science: Non-Statutory Guidance*. York: National Curriculum Council.

Nuffield Primary Science Teachers' Guides (1993). Various titles. London: Collins Educational.

Nuffield (1996) *Primary Science Co-ordinators Handbook*. London: Collins Educational.

Osborne, R. and Freyberg, P. (1985) *Learning in Science*. London: Heinemann.

Peacock, G. (1991) *Floating and Sinking*. Sheffield: Sheffield City Polytechnic/ NES Arnold.

Primary SPACE Project Research Report (1990 – 93). Various titles. Liverpool University Press.

White, R. and Gunstone, R. (1992) *Probing Understanding*. London: Falmer Press.

5
Differentiation in Teaching Science

Stuart Naylor and Brenda Keogh

INTRODUCTION: WHAT IS DIFFERENTIATION IN SCIENCE?

Differentiation has become a very familiar word for teachers. In recent years the National Curriculum and the Ofsted inspection criteria have put pressure on teachers to emphasise differentiation in their planning and in their practice. It would be helpful if there was a single agreed definition for differentiation, but this is not the case.

We feel that Lewis offers a useful start in describing differentiation as 'the process of adjusting teaching to meet the learning needs of individual children' (Lewis, 1992, p. 24). This seems to suggest that teachers should be making conscious decisions about differentiation and that it is an ongoing process. Ofsted offers a slightly different view. Differentiation is 'the matching of work to the differing capabilities of individuals or groups of pupils in order to extend their learning' (Ofsted, 1994, Part 6, p. 27). This definition recognises that planning for differentiation may be for groups as well as for individuals.

This raises a very important issue. Much of the literature is based on the assumption that differentiation is about planning to meet the needs of individual children. This assumption is unrealistic and unhelpful. Although this would be an ideal arrangement, in most classrooms it is not possible for teachers to plan for individual children most of the time. With class sizes as they are, a more realistic approach would be to aim to improve differentiation based upon small groups of children rather than hope to meet the individual needs of the children.

Differentiation in teaching and learning science

Every teacher knows that individual children are different. They vary in their learning capabilities, in their skills and levels of understanding, in their prior experience and in their motivation and commitment. All of these can affect the way that children learn. These differences will be evident in the classroom. Sometimes we may hope that by giving children similar learning experiences we will achieve similar outcomes, but that cannot be guaranteed. More usually the amount and nature of what children learn from the same experience will vary. This could be called differentiation by outcome, and to some extent this can be expected most of the time. However, just because these differences are apparent it does not mean that teaching is differentiated. Differentiation is about 'intervening to make a difference' (Dickinson and Wright, 1993). It is about recognising these differences between children and responding to them appropriately so as to increase the chances of learning taking place.

How can teachers set about intervening to make a difference to children's learning? The obvious way seems to be to match the difficulty of the learning activity to the child's capability. This is usually called differentiation by task. This is certainly worth attempting, but it is difficult! Even in a well-researched area, such as reading, it is far from easy. In science it can be particularly problematic for a variety of reasons. These include the difficulty of ascertaining precisely how learning in science takes place, the problem of identifying how understanding of specific concepts develops and a lack of agreed methods of assessing children's current levels of understanding. The way that the children's existing ideas influence their learning (Nuffield, 1996) also complicates any attempt at matching.

Perhaps it is not surprising that numerous HMI surveys of science teaching point to the difficulties which teachers seem to experience in matching tasks to the children's capabilities, especially for the most able children. However, the demands on teachers have increased dramatically in recent years: Ofsted inspections, a constantly changing National Curriculum and increasing class sizes, to name but a few. If teachers have found matching to be difficult in the past, it is highly unlikely that it will become much easier for them in the future. Finding other approaches to differentiation may therefore be more productive.

ACHIEVING EFFECTIVE DIFFERENTIATION IN LEARNING

Making it manageable

When teachers are already overworked the biggest challenge must be for them to improve differentiation without feeling that they have to dramatically reorganise their classrooms, teach in a completely different way or work even harder! Our experience, and our own research, suggests that many teachers already use quite a wide range of approaches to differentiation. However, we find that it is common for teachers to use a range of approaches yet still feel insecure in how they are addressing differentiation in their teaching. This generally seems to occur when teachers are not explicit about which approach(es) they are using, when they do not make conscious decisions about differentiation and when differentiation does not appear to be included in their planning.

Real progress can be made by reflecting carefully on how differentiation is tackled and by becoming more aware of what approaches are already in use. This will help to make the existing practice which may be intuitive more evident. By making more conscious decisions at the planning stage about which approaches to use it is possible to differentiate more effectively and to feel more confident that progress is being made. The reality for many teachers is that differentiation can be improved without adding significantly to the workload in the long term.

Making it applicable to all children

Sometimes differentiation is viewed as something which is only necessary for 'special' children, such as those with identified learning difficulties (Russell et al, 1994). Often their learning needs will be significantly different from those of the other children in the class. One obvious approach to differentiation is to plan one activity for the whole class or group, with an alternative for these children if they are unable to cope. However, this approach runs the risk that other children will not really be challenged and that their learning needs will not be met. When some children are not sufficiently challenged the only evidence may be that they are successful in the activity! The problem of insufficient challenge may be much more difficult to spot than the problem of too great a challenge.

More effective differentiation will attempt to take the learning needs of all the children into account, not just some (Visser, 1993). Differentiation must be seen as relevant to all the children, not just to those at the extremes in terms of ability, motivation or behaviour. However, the difficulties of predicting how an individual child will interact with a particular activity will be familiar to teachers. Attempting to get the degree of challenge right must not become an intolerable burden for teachers. Using a range of teaching and learning styles and adopting a flexible approach to planning and organisation will go some way to meeting the needs of all of the children. Viewing plans as provisional and adjusting the activity and learning environment in the light of the children's responses will help to ensure that the activity is accessible and challenging to all the children (Harlen, 1985).

Making differentiation a shared responsibility
Although teachers can plan for differentiation, their plans may not always work out in practice. The purpose of differentiation is to maximise learning, and however carefully the teacher plans the children's learning, it cannot always be prescribed in advance. The children also have an important role and they share the responsibility for learning with the teacher. If they are determined not to learn then they won't!

Clearly the teacher must always retain ultimate responsibility for what happens in the classroom. However, the more the children can be encouraged to become aware of and involved in their learning, the more effective differentiation can become. Children who are willing partners in learning will offer the teacher more opportunity to find out their views, to adjust activities by taking their responses into account and to negotiate the most suitable programme of activities.

Not all children are ready to be willing partners in learning, and that in itself is a challenge for many teachers. When children are disruptive or lacking in motivation differentiation may not be the first priority. There are no simple solutions to the complex problems of children being unwilling to learn. Nevertheless, we have experienced many instances where giving the children greater responsibility in their learning has led to increased involvement, greater motivation and more effective learning.

STRATEGIES

Differentiating in the classroom
Differentiation by task and differentiation by outcome have already been mentioned. Fortunately, they are not the only strategies which are available to teachers. Outlines of possible strategies are provided by various authors, including Stradling and Saunders (1992), NCC

(1993) and Naylor and Keogh (1995). The strategies suggested offer support for evaluating the range of approaches in use currently, identifying how opportunities for differentiation can be built into planning and considering how the level of demand of an activity might be adjusted.

Many of these strategies involve responding during an activity. It would be a mistake to assume that differentiation only happens before (planning for differentiation by task) or at the end of (differentiation by outcome) an activity. In practice the use of a range of differentiation strategies while the children are working may be the most important aspect of differentiation.

Using a range of learning styles
The same content might be covered in different ways by different children (eg through researching in texts, through a practical investigation, through a structured workcard or through a computer simulation). This may occur in an unplanned way when children are having difficulties with an activity and the teacher suggests an alternative approach.

Building on the children's ideas
Clearly it is necessary for teachers to plan activities. However, if the children can be given the opportunity to contribute their ideas then the purpose of the planned activity can be to test out their ideas. This can help to ensure that they all see the activity as purposeful and meaningful.

Adjusting the level of demand of a task during the activity
The children's responses to an activity will provide information to the teacher about how suitable that activity is. It may then be possible to adjust the demand of the activity where necessary to make it either more accessible for some children or more challenging for others.

Adjusting the level of scientific skills required
Although the children may be working with the same concepts, the nature of any investigation that they carry out may vary. A more sophisticated investigation will be more demanding than a straightforward investigation involving fewer factors.

Varying the distribution of teacher time
Some children may be targeted for extra attention at certain times. This will probably happen automatically to some extent.

Differentiation can be more effective when there is some degree of planning about how time will be distributed. Support teachers and parents may also be involved in providing this additional attention.

Varying the amount and nature of teacher intervention
The degree of support, guidance, challenge and monitoring can be adjusted for individuals and groups; this can also happen automatically. Becoming more aware of the intuitive decisions being made will make differentiation in this respect more effective.

Varying the degree of independence expected of the children
Having responsibility for additional decisions will generally make an activity more demanding. Science investigations provide a rich source of possible opportunities for children to take responsibility for making relevant decisions details can be found in Jarman, Keogh and Naylor (1994).

Careful use of questioning
This can help to identify individual needs as well as offer additional challenges. Targeting more straightforward or more challenging questions to certain children is a skill which many teachers use with great subtlety. Useful guidance on questioning is given by Harlen (1992).

Varying the response expected
Some children can be expected to produce more detailed or more complex responses than others. This could include an answer to a question, a plan for an investigation, the type of observation or measurement made, the length and quality of a written report, how findings are communicated, and so on. Managing discussion so that all children's contributions are valued is also a skill at which many teachers excel.

Varying the pace of learning
The children may cover the same sequence of activities by working at different rates. Some children can be set a more demanding schedule than others; some children may need additional support to complete the set of activities.

Varying the method of presentation
The same ideas may be presented in different ways to different children (eg as a challenge, as a question or as a procedure to follow). Sometimes it may be possible to give the children a choice of methods

of gaining access to an activity so that their own preferences can be taken into account.

Varying the method of recording
Different children may analyse, record and present their experimental data in different ways. The amount of detail required, the degree of accuracy or the level of quantification can influence how demanding this will be.

Adjusting the level of linguistic demand
This can apply to both written and oral language, where factors such as the complexity of the language, the use of scientific vocabulary, the use of pictorial representation and the use of everyday analogy can vary. All of these can make the activity more or less demanding.

Adjusting the level of mathematical demand
Factors such as the degree of precision, the scale, the level of quantification and the use of symbols or units can vary. Presenting data often requires mathematical and/or graphical skills. All these factors can influence the degree of challenge in an activity.

Providing a range of resources
Access to support materials such as reference texts, visual images, pre-recorded tapes, extension worksheets or concept (overlay) key-boards can vary according to the children's needs and experience. A systematic approach to obtaining and generating suitable resource material can produce long-term benefits.

Choosing appropriate strategies
Having a list of strategies can be an important step in making decisions about differentiation more explicit. It is unlikely that all of these strategies will be used at any one time, so having a list doesn't remove the need to make decisions. However, with such a list, the process of making decisions can become more systematic and manageable. Any decision about which approach(es) might be most suitable will be influenced by the circumstances at the time. These will include:

- the range of abilities and learning needs in the group;

- the children's behaviour (sometimes this can be the overriding factor);

- the resources available, including texts, IT and in-class support;

- the time available.

Clearly there can be no single answer as to which approach is best. However, in all aspects of classroom life teachers are expected to use their professional judgement in making difficult decisions. Differentiation is no exception. There is no guarantee that any individual decision will be the right one, but a reflective approach and a willingness to learn from experience will make the right decisions more likely.

There is a lot to be said for trying out approaches that may be unfamiliar in order to gain experience of as wide a range of teaching and learning approaches as possible. Children will benefit from variety and they can be given the opportunity to reflect on what learning style is most suitable for them. This can be an important aspect of making learning a shared responsibility.

It is also important to be explicit about what approaches to differentiation are being adopted. For individual teachers it will help to ensure that opportunities for differentiated learning are identified and made use of where possible. For the school as a whole it will help to ensure that a common understanding is reached and that there is continuity of approach from year to year.

Creating circumstances which will support differentiation

In addition to the strategies suggested above, there are other, more general, steps that teachers can take to promote differentiation. Fortunately none of them require additional resources and they are all manageable in ordinary classrooms.

Actively involve children in their own learning

We mentioned earlier that differentiation in learning has to be seen as a shared responsibility, in which the teacher's responsibility for planning and organising activities is complemented by the children's involvement in taking an active role in their own learning. Attempting to enhance the children's involvement in learning will naturally lead to the use of active learning methods as the typical approach. Frequently this will involve practical activities, though not always. Bentley and Watts (1989) and Fisher (1990) provide useful illustrations of a range of active learning methods.

Active involvement can also be fostered by sharing intentions for their learning with the children, by constantly providing opportunities for them to make significant decisions about their learning and by encouraging them to reflect on their learning. Through active involvement children will come to understand that differentiation is a process negotiated with the teacher rather than something forced upon them by the teacher.

Establish classroom routines that maximise the children's independence as learners

Independent learning should not be confused with individual learning. In fact children working successfully as independent learners will inevitably be working collaboratively for much of the time. Neither should it be taken to mean that children can do exactly what they want.

Independent learning in the classroom will have several different facets. These include the more obvious aspects, such as access to information and to resources. They also include the range of decisions that need to be made in the classroom, such as the order of activities, the time scale involved, the details of the procedure, what information to record, how to present information, what to communicate and so on. Although it is unlikely that children will be involved in all of these different aspects at any one time, they all provide opportunities for the children to act as independent learners.

The opportunities offered to any particular group will depend on factors such as their age, their previous experience and their level of involvement. Although it may be tempting to think that independence can only be aimed for with the oldest or most able children, this is not the case in practice (Russell et al, 1994). Like any behaviour, independence needs to be learnt. Opportunities for developing such behaviours and skills therefore need to be created. Where there is a whole-school commitment to this way of working, the levels of independence of very young children can be surprising.

Whatever the mechanism, it is the outcome that is important. The more independent the children are, the more time the teacher can spend on monitoring, supporting and challenging them rather than simply organising them. Differentiation depends on effective interaction with the children. Children working as independent learners enables this to occur.

Create a supportive classroom climate

A supportive classroom climate provides a basis for effective differentiation (NCC, 1989). Classroom climate influences relationships, communication, interaction, motivation and involvement; in short it provides many of the things upon which differentiation depends. When children have the confidence to speak freely because they know that their ideas will be regarded as worthwhile, then communication will be more open and more productive.

Classroom climate is not easy to describe. Perhaps 'person-centred' is the most useful description. It describes a classroom in which individuals are valued, in which there is effective communication and co-operation and in which empathy and affirmation are evident. Classrooms such as these do not just happen by accident. Creating and sustaining this kind of learning environment requires a range of interpersonal and professional skills in the teacher. It also requires a lot of patience, since building up positive working relationships in the classroom always takes time.

Work towards a whole-school approach

The importance of some degree of continuity in a school's approach to differentiation cannot be overstated. Many of the strategies suggested above rely heavily on interaction and communication with the children and require the teacher to adopt certain roles. Interaction and communication cannot be as effective as they might be if roles and expectations change dramatically from one teacher to the next. By contrast, where there is continuity in roles and expectations from one teacher to another, relationships will be more secure, communication will be more effective and the scope for negotiating learning arrangements with the children will be greater.

Of course, decisions about whether to adopt a whole-school approach to differentiation will be made by the whole-school team, not by individual teachers. Individual teachers may have some influence on these decisions through their relationships with the children, through informal contact with other members of staff and through more formal structures such as staff meetings. Sometimes it is necessary to accept that consistency of approach across the staff will not be achieved in the short to medium term, and that a whole-school approach must remain a long-term aim. However, even if it proves unattainable in practice, it is a goal worth aiming for.

EVALUATION

Evaluating progress in differentiation in science

This chapter has attempted to map out some of the strategies which can be helpful for putting differentiation into practice and some general pointers towards making differentiation in science teaching and learning more likely. Each of these could be used as an indicator of progress in differentiation by an individual teacher or by a school.

Being able to make approaches to differentiation explicit can in itself be an indicator of progress.

The list of possible strategies provides an obvious opportunity to evaluate the approaches which are being used currently: which of these strategies are used at the moment; how frequently are they used; do teachers know which strategies are in use at any time and could any of them be used more effectively?

The pointers towards making differentiation more likely provide a similar kind of opportunity: which of them can be identified in the classroom; which of them are widespread across the school; and is there any consensus about whole-school approaches to teaching and learning?

These issues will be taken up in Book 2, where the emphasis will be on in-service activities for teachers to support reflecting on and extending existing practice.

BIBLIOGRAPHY

Bentley, D. and Watts, M. (1989) *Learning and Teaching in School Science: Practical Alternatives*. Milton Keynes: Open University Press.

Dickinson, C. and Wright, J. (1993) *Differentiation: A Practical Handbook of Classroom Strategies*. Coventry: National Council for Educational Technology.

Fisher, R. (1990) *Teaching Children to Think*. Hemel Hempstead: Simon and Schuster.

Harlen, W. (1985) *Teaching and Learning Primary Science*. London: Harper and Row.

Harlen, W. (1992) *The Teaching of Science*. London: David Fulton.

Jarman, R., Keogh, B. and Naylor, S. (1994) *I've Done This Before: Continuity and Progression in School Science*. Hatfield: Association for Science Education.

Lewis, A. (1992) From Planning to Practice. *British Journal of Special Education*, vol. 19, no. 1, pp. 24–7.

Naylor, S. and Keogh, B. (1995) Making Differentiation Manageable. *School Science Review*, vol. 76, no. 279, pp. 106–110.

National Curriculum Council (1989) *Curriculum Guidance 2: A Curriculum for All*. York: National Curriculum Council.

National Curriculum Council (1993) *Teaching Science at Key Stages 1 and 2*. York: National Curriculum Council.

Nuffield (1996) *Primary Science Co-ordinator's Handbook*. London: Collins Educational.

Office for Standards in Education (Ofsted) (1994) *Handbook for the Inspection of Schools*. London: HMSO.

Russell, R. et al (1994) *Evaluation of the Implementation of Science in the*

National Curriculum at Key Stages 1, 2 and 3. Volume 3: Differentiation. London: School Curriculum and Assessment Authority.

Stradling, B. and Saunders, L. (1993) Differentiation in Practice: Responding to the Needs of all Pupils. *Educational Research*, vol. 35, pp. 127–37.

Visser, J. (1993) *Differentiation: Making It Work*. Stafford: National Association for Special Educational Needs.

6
Equal Opportunities and the Teaching of Science

Gill Peet

INTRODUCTION AND BACKGROUND

Few primary teachers in the United Kingdom would deny that equality of opportunity is one of the most important issues facing education today. However, understanding of the issue is somewhat varied and the reasons for addressing equality in individual schools are not always the same. Entwistle (1978) has defined equality as the 'removal of hindrances to the development of individual talent'. Recognition of the nature of these hindrances is subjective and forms part of the debate.

Through the example of racial and cultural equality, which typifies the complexity of the issues, this chapter seeks to exemplify an approach to equal opportunities. The first step is to establish an understanding of the 'issues' in the wider context.

The area of racial equality has for many years been the subject of much educational discussion. The arrival in this country in the 1950s and 1960s of visibly recognisable immigrants focused attention on the variety of cultural and ethnic backgrounds of children in school. Previously the only type of equality to have been addressed in any real way was social equality which provided the rationale, during the last century and throughout this century, for 'schooling for all'. Even this movement was confined to the extension of opportunity rather than equality which some would say has yet to be achieved.

Although immigrants have always been a part of British culture, their arrival was, until the post-war years, usually ignored and they were expected to pick up the English language and take steps to assimilate themselves into the 'English' culture. In the 1950s and the 1960s their increase in numbers necessitated special consideration and the response was to provide provision, under Section 11 of the Local Government Act 1966, to develop English as a second language. The notion of providing equality of opportunity was not paramount, the emphasis being on provision to enable teachers to cope and promote assimilation. In the latter part of this century the idea of multicultural education developed in which teachers started to consider that an education which reflected the culture and beliefs of all children would help all of them respond more positively to the changes happening within society. Schools began to recognise the customs and festivals of different cultures but still with a focus on diminishing the differences between groups.

It was only in the 1980s that there was any widespread recognition that this was often tokenism and that many children from ethnic minority communities were suffering from the consequences of racism. The Rampton Committee (1981), set up to investigate the under-achievement of West Indian children, claimed that teacher attitudes and racism were important factors contributing to the under-achievement of black pupils. The Swann Report (1985), which grew from the work of the Rampton Committee, accepted this claim and extended the notion of multicultural education by introducing one of 'cultural pluralism' which was that all cultures should be valued equally and that this should be taught to children in school. The rationale for this was that racism was caused by some sort of cultural ignorance or misunderstanding. Most teachers readily accepted this proposition and endeavoured to respond. In practice, however, they themselves operated from a cultural point of view that was their own, typically white and middle class and often without sufficient under-standing or knowledge to provide anything but a token examination of other cultures. Rarely did they ever draw upon the real lives and experiences of the children being taught and their teaching did little to challenge racial disadvantage. It was at this point that a distinction started to appear between multicultural education and anti-rascist education.

Prejudice and discrimination

The Scarman Report (1981) on the riots in Brixton of 1981 had earlier concluded that 'racial disadvantage is a fact of current British life (and) was . . . a significant factor in the causation of the Brixton disorders.' Lord Swann (1985) recognised this and identified the need to combat prejudice which his Committee perceived as being at the root of the problem.

Prejudice was defined in the Swann report as 'preconceived opinion or bias for or against someone or something'. It operates through a common process of stereotyping and devaluation which has the effect of legitimising discrimination against specific groups and thus maintaining the advantages of the majority by limiting the opportunities of the specific group or groups being discriminated against. Although the focus of concern of the Swann report was largely directed at racial prejudice, we can now recognise that prejudice may encompass gender, disability, social class or indeed be manifested against any person or group of people who are at variance with the attributes of the majority. In fact, the report of the Macdonald Enquiry (Manchester City Council, 1988) into racism and racial violence in Manchester schools expressly stated that 'We do not believe that an effective anti-racist policy can exist unless the other issues are also addressed and dealt with, in particular class and gender.'

The role of education

What then do we mean when we talk about equal opportunities in the context of education? We should be wary of a word like 'equality'. It suggests that all people are the same, but is this true? Individuals have different aspirations and live in different circumstances. It is not enough simply to treat people in the same way. Differences have to be recognised and addressed. Teachers have a responsibility to be aware of all forms of injustice that may be operating to the disadvantage of their pupils, how such disadvantage operates to create educational inequalities in access and outcome and a responsibility to develop the skills and knowledge to act effectively for equality. The purpose of this chapter is to show how we can work towards providing a primary science education which gives every child equal opportunity to succeed regardless of race, gender, socio-economic class or disability. Such an approach should be extended to any other identifiable group so that no child in the primary school is disadvantaged at an early age from later either pursuing a career in science and technology or from using science as part of their lives in work or as citizens.

a scientist

Girl 11

a scientist

Boy 11

Fig. 8. Children's images of scientists

CHALLENGES: RECOGNISING THAT CHILDREN CAN BE DISEMPOWERED IN SCIENCE

Attitudes to science

When a science curriculum fails to address prejudice and stereotyping, all children are disempowered. Many teachers assume that education is free from bias, empowering all children equally according to their ability (Jeffcoate, 1979). There is a similar view that science is neutral (Farrell, 1990). In order to recognise the issue of equality, we need to examine more closely our own and society's popular perspectives of scientists and scientific inventions which are likely to influence the attitudes of teachers and of the children we are teaching and their progress in science.

Society's perception of science

The notion of neutrality in science and the related perception that science is culture-free leads to the view that there is therefore no role for science in working towards a society free from prejudice. This perception could be attributed to the fact that school science rarely recognises the contributions made beyond Europe and thus encourages a Eurocentric view of science (Cross and Pearce, 1993). If we examine research into children's views of scientists (see Figure 8) we see that their perception is that scientists are white and male and that all scientific discoveries are Western European (Newton and Newton, 1991).

If we only talk about western science in our teaching we are perpetuating this myth and encouraging the stereotype of an inferior person who is not European, white and male. It is interesting to consider how many black or women scientists you can name or how many inventions you know that come from non-European or black countries. We need to acknowledge that science is the inheritance of all people. As societies have developed differently so also has science differed from place to place. 'Children need to be taught the fact that science and technology are not exclusively white, European and male phenomena' (Siraj-Blatchford and Siraj-Blatchford, 1991).

Children's attitudes to culture and science

There is a body of opinion amongst teachers of early years that young children do not see the colour of skin (Jeffcoate, 1979). Research has shown, however, that even five-year-olds are capable of having disparaging views of minority groups. In 1974 and 1975 the Schools Council/NFER project, Education for a Multiracial Society, researched the implications for the curriculum of living in a multiracial society. Although research confirmed the early onset of racial attitudes, almost all of the headteachers involved with the project rejected the findings as being inapplicable to their own schools and insisted that young children in their schools were oblivious of race and that the different ethnic groups mixed and played together. As a result of this impasse, several of the schools involved subjected themselves to a more rigorous examination of the children's racial attitudes. All were surprised to find that their views were wrong and that a considerable degree of racism existed. This appeared to stem from stereotyped images of black people and third world countries. When a situation was set up in which nursery children could express views freely, unhindered by the protocol of the normal nursery routine, even they were found to have strong views about skin colour and race (Jeffcoate, 1979). In 1983 David Milner showed through his research that children as young as three could not only distinguish between different skin colours but could give different values to them.

STRATEGIES FOR ENSURING EQUALITY IN PRIMARY SCIENCE

As teachers we need to be aware of the two strands that have to be considered when providing equality of opportunity. These are, firstly, to ensure that the education provided is itself equally accessible to all children, and secondly, to ensure that the children being taught learn to recognise that they have equal opportunities to succeed and that all others, regardless of their background, share this right to equal opportunities. This right to equal opportunities is enriched by the responsibility we all share to ensure that such rights are enjoyed by all.

Ensuring curriculum access for all

Our view of science will determine the sort of science we teach. If we perceive science as being a set of truths or facts which can and should be learnt by rote then the child experiencing difficulties with English will necessarily be disadvantaged. Memorising facts is difficult for many learners because it is seen as not relevant and not real and it is often not required to be linked to understanding. For children with a poor command of English such learning is impossible. In Chapter 3 Dave Heywood stresses the important place of language in concept formation. If, however, we see science as being a way of developing skills and each person's understanding of the world then there are strategies we can use to empower all children.

Children who frequently experience failure develop low self-esteem. Practical work in science enables all children to take part and helps to remove such barriers to learning. If everyday situations are used, relevance to the child's own life is more easily perceived. Practical work is, however, more than simply a device to enable all children to 'take part.' An approach which concentrates on the practical and cognitive processes of science is seen by many modern science educationalists as the most effective method of allowing all children to develop understanding of scientific concepts. Harlen (1993, p. 135) suggests that 'Process-based learning in science is likely to project a more human view of science and to involve learning experiences that engage the thinking, imagination and interest of pupils as well as leading to an understanding of key concepts and principles.' She also claims that although 'process learning is not designed to appeal to girls and women . . . the argument has been advanced that it does' (ibid, p. 135).

For children experiencing difficulties with English, working with a more fluent partner can help to facilitate understanding and increase involvement.

Heavy reliance on a workcard approach to science will obviously disadvantage children who have reading difficulties; therefore the use of primary science schemes should be considered carefully. Research done by Peacock (1995) suggests that 'a science scheme has as yet not been produced in the UK which has deliberately and successfully taken account of the needs of L2 (English as a second language) children.' Furthermore, a constant demand to present results in written form will not enhance learning in science but distract from it and demotivate the learner. A solution to this problem is to display results pictorially and to present them as a classroom display.

Developing awareness throughout the school

The development of awareness of prejudice is as much, if not more, the concern of the so-called middle class all-white school as it is of the inner-city, multi-ethnic school and is in some respects even more fundamental in the former. We need to be aware of the insidious effect of stereotyping and the prejudice that develops from it. Only by becoming aware of our own prejudices can we start to build a curriculum that attacks the roots of prejudice. We also may have to recognise that some of our actions are unintentionally racist. There will always be a minority of teachers whose behaviour is motivated by malice but there are others whose actions are simply thoughtless or ignorant (Jeffcoate, 1979). Such behaviour may emanate from ignorance of the background of the children they are teaching. It should not be assumed that people from other cultures will do things in the way people from our own culture do them. The conduct of everyday activities regarded as 'normal' by some may be conducted quite differently by others. 'For example, a common British custom is to make tea by boiling a kettle then pouring the boiling water over the tea leaves in a teapot. Some Asian children may make tea by boiling the water and tea together in a pan on the hob' (Cross and Pearce, 1993). We should also be aware of the restrictions that religion may put upon the children in our class as well as the cultural traditions of simply doing things differently. It is important that we know our children well and are informed about their culture.

Developing an equal opportunities science curriculum
Clearly, if strategies for introducing all pupils to science are to be effective there has to be an agreed school policy to which every teacher has contributed and with which all are agreed. For such a policy to be successful it should meet the following criteria.

1. Be both culturally diverse in its choice of content and put science into a real world context where different viewpoints are considered and stereotypes challenged.

   News programmes perpetuate the myth that everyone in Africa is starving whereas science can help children challenge this. A study of the food imported from other countries can form part of a wider topic on food. The science could include an investigation into how different crops require varying conditions for growth and why a particular country, say Southern Africa and its oranges, may be more able to supply this crop than we are. Such an investigation provides a stimulating change to the traditional work on growth often done with beans or cress. Likewise a study of animal life and life processes can be extended to a consideration of the specific needs of animals from other countries which enable them to survive successfully in an environment different from our own. For example, the constraints upon the dispersal of animal life provided by the walls of the Ngorongoro crater mean that there is sufficient food for the predators.

   Diets from other cultures could be examined in order for children to understand that other foods, although very different in appearance and presentation, can nevertheless provide a healthy and balanced diet. Some of the meat products which may seem strange or even unpleasant to indigenous children could be compared to some of their own more unusual eating habits, such as the eating of offal and the high blood content of black puddings.

2. Recognise and value the contributions made to science from people of other cultures and backgrounds to our own.

   The story of Charles Richard Drew is particularly poignant and will appeal to many children. Drew was a black American scientist who developed blood banks as a way of keeping blood available for transfusions. Ironically, when Drew was involved in a car accident in Alabama the hospital refused to take him because they did not accept black people. Although they were using his techniques in the hospital, their refusal to supply him with the blood transfusion he needed cost him his life.

   Other black scientists include Elijah J. McCoy who invented a device for lubricating locomotive engines that was so good that buyers only wanted 'the real McCoy'.

   Women scientists include not only Marie Curie but also Caroline Herschel, who after her brother William discovered the planet Uranus, went on herself to discover eight comets and became the first woman to be made an honorary member of the Royal Society (Reiss, 1993). It is interesting to be aware that many other women scientists remain unknown because their work was often published under the name of another and their contributions not recognised.

   A look at some of the early inventions of the Chinese such as 'the compass, deep drilling for natural gas, the suspension bridge, paper, biological pest control, Newton's (sic) First Law' (Temple, 1991) will destroy the myth that everything of any value was invented or discovered in Western Europe or America.

3. Ensure that textbooks used do not contain discriminatory stereotyping. Many textbooks now include illustrations of people from other cultures but we should look carefully at what they are doing. Are they doing the inferior menial tasks? Are they dressed in a way that is giving a particular message? Are women portrayed in capable roles? Are the girls playing house and the boys flying aircraft?

4. Ensure that we have equally high expectations of all the children in our class regardless of gender, race or social class.

5. Ensure that the language we use does not make science inaccessible to any particular child or group of children.

6. Teach science that is relevant to the children. It has long been accepted that we should start with the familiar and proceed gradually to the unknown (Inhelder and Piaget, 1966; Ausubel, 1968).

   In order to do this we need ourselves to know more about the background of the children we are teaching. Areas of particular cultural sensitivity include food, life processes, clothing, relationships and cultural traditions (Cross and Pearce, 1993). Food is a particularly popular topic in the primary curriculum but we need to be aware not only of the range and diversity of the foods that children from ethnic minority groups might be eating but also of the religious restrictions attached to some foods. Similarly children from a poor family may not have the same awareness of the range of foods eaten by others, as children from more affluent homes.

7. Be sensitive (but not biased) to the needs of disadvantaged children.

8. Assessment should be sensitive and avoid any bias. It is important that assessment recognises the real progress a pupil is making and assessment tasks themselves should not therefore be presented in a way that disadvantages any child; for example, by presenting a child with a workcard which the child cannot read. Children with poorly developed reading and writing ability in English should be able to present their ideas orally and pictorially.

9. Ensure that teachers are aware of the role model they present and of their own stereotyped images. In most primary schools the majority of teaching staff are female. Their own attitudes to science and technology will contribute towards the stereotyped image of women that children are developing and may influence the attitudes of the children to science.

10. Stress the similarities as much as the differences between all cultures and groups.

11. Ensure that activities are differentiated to ensure access for all children (Chapter 5).

Planning activities with equal opportunities in mind

Science offers a unique opportunity to combine practical skills with mathematical and language skills. Even when language is poorly developed, success can still be achieved. With careful introduction by the teacher, children can investigate phenomena and demonstrate their findings without the need for a sophisticated use of language whilst at the same time using the activity as a means and motivation for developing their language skills.

In Chapter 2, Linda McGuigan and Mike Schilling advocate a constructivist approach to science teaching and learning and to the active involvement of the learner in the whole process. Contrary to what we might at first think, this view of learning is not inaccessible to children with English as a second language, but is actually a means of making the science more relevant to them as individuals. Even with only limited English, the learner can become involved in testing their own ideas through investigations. Process skills such as observing, predicting, interpreting and hypothesising can all be developed in this way. This not only satisfies the procedural requirements of the National Curriculum but is also a more effective way of learning science.

Activities should be planned which:

- include content that is seen by the learner to be useful, relevant and of practical use;
- are based on daily experiences with which the learner can identify;
- enable the learner to understand more of themselves and of the key concepts in science;
- appeal to children of different cultures, of both genders and of all social groups;
- emphasise a process approach to learning which will encourage understanding.

All activities should then be checked to:

- see if there is the potential within them to include a multicultural dimension;
- ensure that there is no inadvertent prejudice or stereotyping;
- consider whether there is the opportunity to use the activity to actively work against stereotyping and prejudice;
- ensure that teaching strategies allow all pupils regardless of class, culture or gender to have equal opportunity to participate.

National Curriculum	Activity	Opportunity for multicultural content	Avoiding prejudice and stereotyping
	Looking at a wide range of clothes	Ensure that clothes from other cultures are included. Name and label them using appropriate language to describe the clothes	Encouraging respect for difference by discussing reasons why clothes are different, eg religion, climate, etc.
AT1 PoS 1,2,3	Investigation into the most suitable colour for wearing to stay cool	Looking at why white is often worn in hot countries	Respecting and valuing the judgements of others
	Investigation into the best material for keeping warm	Thinking about the use of animal skins in cold countries	Accepting that we also use leather for clothes

Fig. 9.   Key Stage 1 topic on clothes

Examples of activities children might do
Clothes
When looking at a range of clothes ask children to bring in their favourite clothes. Name and label them using appropriate language wherever possible. If there are no children from an ethnic minority group, bring in some clothes yourself or bring in a doll or a picture displaying a variety of clothes. Discuss reasons for wearing clothes: for example, to comply with society's expectations, to keep warm, or to comply with religious requirements. Discuss the countries where the clothes are worn and their different climatic conditions: for example, the need to keep cool whilst still being covered up. One investigation could be to discover which colours absorb heat and which reflect it most effectively. Add an ice cube to each of two dolls and cover one with black cloth and one with white cloth. Examine the dolls

National Curriculum	Activity	Opportunity for multicultural content	Avoiding prejudice and stereotyping
AT3 PoS 2b – Changing materials when they are heated or cooled.	Cooking	Looking at different cooking pots, eg pans, woks, balti dishes, earthenware pots, etc.	Not valuing one method more than another. Looking at the range of methods used in any one culture
AT2 PoS 3a; 5a,b	Growing seeds	Growing not only cress but also such things as coriander and moong beans	Recognising that our choice of foods has been affected by our ability to produce it

Fig. 10. Key Stage 1 topic on food

at intervals to see which ice cube melts first. Investigations done practically in this way with young children help them all, especially those with poorly developed English, to understand the nature and purpose of the activity.

The multicultural content is added by extending the investigation to cover clothes from other ethnic groups and identifying not only differences but similarities. Stereotyping is addressed by identifying reasons for the differences and the often logical development of customs.

This can be reinforced when developing investigative skills through testing materials for their suitability for their purpose: for example, testing to find out which is the most suitable material for keeping people cool in hot countries, warm in cold countries, protected when doing particular work, etc (see Figure 9).

Food

Food is eaten by everybody and is a useful way of both making science relevant and emphasising the similarities between people of different cultures (see Figure 10).

Instead of simply looking at the different foods that are eaten, look also at the way foods are preserved. In many hot countries foods are dried; for example, desiccated coconut, Bombay duck (dried bumalo fish), meat and spices. Even in cold countries fish is sometimes wind

National Curriculum	Activity	Opportunity for multicultural content	Avoiding prejudice and stereotyping
AT1 PoS 1,2 3. AT2 PoS 1a,2b, 5a,5e	Preserving different foods	Looking at the ways in which food is preserved in other countries	Recognising that we utilise the best methods that are available to us, and that the final product is tasty and nutritious food

Fig. 11. Key Stage 2 topic on food

dried. Pickling is a common way of preserving food but the choice of vinegar (malt, wine, lemon juice) depends on the availability. This has led to a range of different tasting preserves. In this country we have a tradition of bottling fruit and vegetables or of making them into jams. Most people preserve milk by turning it into cheese or yoghurt. Children can combine cookery with science by attempting to preserve foods in different ways or investigate cheese-making in different parts of the world (see Figure 11).

Electricity and magnetism

Electricity and magnetism may seem to be subjects that are value- and culture-free, but even here there is room to develop awareness as can be seen in Figure 12. Hence, teachers should constantly seek oppor-

National Curriculum	Activity	Opportunity for multicultural content	Avoiding prejudice and stereotyping
AT4 PoS 1. (c) Ways of varying the current to make bulbs brighter or dimmer	Setting up circuits and changing various components		Learning that although Edison invented the light bulb, it was a Black American, Latimer, who invented one that could last for longer than a week

Fig. 12. Key Stage 2 topic on electricity and magnetism

tunities to reinforce the fact that science belongs to us all and Europeans do not have a monopoly on scientific inventions.

EVALUATING SUCCESS

Recognising issues of prejudice and making plans to remedy them is not in itself enough. If we do not constantly evaluate what we are doing, good intentions remain thwarted and traditional practice continues. The following checklist may be useful for monitoring our own progress and reminding us of the need for constant positive action in order to provide equal opportunities for all.

Checklist for teachers
1. Do you know about the background of the children in your class?
2. How much do you know about their culture?
3. Do you ensure that you have avoided a Eurocentric view of science and have added a multicultural dimension wherever possible?
4. Do you check to ensure that activities do not encourage stereotyping and prejudice?
5. Do you have a whole-school policy for developing equal opportunities in science?
6. Do you ensure that science activities are accessible to all? Are they set within the experience of the children? Is the language accessible or is an alternative approach used? Are the activities process-based and not only language-based?
7. Are we sensitive to ourselves as role models?
8. Do we ensure that assessment tasks are accessible to all? Are they dependent on language skills or familiarity with a foreign culture or is the task one that is traditionally favoured by one sex or the other? We must guard against our own prejudices influencing our perceptions of appropriate behaviour.

CONCLUSION

That science is part of the Core Curriculum (DFE, 1995) is an indication of the current importance given to developing a scientifically literate society. Not only do pupils need to be able to make sense of their world in order to cope with their lives, but society needs both trained scientists and technologists. I have already referred to Harlen's claim (1993) when referring to women that 'it would not be possible to foster a scientifically literate population when half of that population is under-achieving in their science education.' If we further add the pupils who are under-achieving because of culture, class or disability we are left with a small minority of scientifically literate people. This is a serious position to be in and for the future we cannot afford to deny access to science to any part of our society.

Nor can we be complacent in thinking that prejudice is not a problem. Current figures suggest that the number of racist incidents is still rising. This is related to the perception, which stems from prejudice, that anyone with an image different from our own is necessarily inferior or a threat. We need in our teaching to portray all members of our society as being equally valuable human beings, and as teachers we need to remember that we are not only concerned with multicultural and gender prejudice but that class prejudice is one of the most insidious forms of discrimination affecting children in our society today. Our science teaching can help to develop tolerance through understanding and equal opportunity for all, through examination by children of the contributions of women and those from other cultures, through discussions on values, and our world commitment to preserving our environment.

BIBLIOGRAPHY

Ausubel, D. (1968) *Educational Psychology*. New York: Holt, Rinehart and Winston.

Cross, A. and Pearce, G. (1993) Core Subject Science, in P. Pumfrey and G. K. Verma, (eds.) *Cultural Diversity and the Curriculum Vol. 3*. London: The Falmer Press.

Department for Education (1995) *Key Stages One and Two of the National Curriculum*. London: HMSO.

Entwistle, J. (1978) *Class, Culture and Education*. London: Methuen.

Farrell, P. (1990) *Multicultural Education*. Leamington Spa: Scholastic Publications.

Harlen, W. (1993) Education for Equal Opportunities in a Scientifically Literate Society, in E. Whitelegg, J. Thomas and S. Tresman (eds.) *Challenges and Opportunities for Science Education*. London: The Open University/Paul Chapman Publishing Ltd.

Inhelder, B. and Piaget, J. (1958) *The Growth of Logical Thinking from Childhood to Adolescence*. London: Routledge & Kegan Paul.

Jeffcoate, R. (1979) *Positive Image: Towards a Multiracial Curriculum*. Richmond: Chameleon Books.

Manchester City Council (1988) *Burnage Inquiry: Extract of Report for Public Use*. Manchester City Council.

Milner, D. (1983) *Children and Race: Ten Years On*. London: Penguin.

Newton, L. D. and Newton, D. (1991) Child's View of a Scientist. *Questions*, vol. 4 (no. 1), pp. 20–1.

Peacock, A. (1995) The Use of Primary Science Schemes with Second Language Learners. *Primary Science Review*, vol. 38, pp. 14–15.

Rampton Report (1981) *West Indian Children in our Schools: Interim Report of the Committee of Inquiry into the Education of Children from Ethnic Minority Groups*. Cmnd. 8273. London: HMSO.

Reiss, M. (1993) *Science Education for a Pluralist Society*. Buckingham: Open University Press.

Siraj-Blatchford, I. and Siraj-Blatchford, J. (1991) Science and Cultural Relevance. *Primary Science Review*, vol. 17, pp. 16–17.

Scarman Report (1981) *The Brixton Disorders*. Cmnd 8427. London: HMSO.

Swann Report (1985) *Education for All: The Report of the Committee of Inquiry into the Education of Children from Ethnic Minority Groups*. Cmnd. 9453. London: HMSO.

Temple, R. (1991) *The Genius of China: 3000 Years of Science, Discovery and Invention*. London: Prion/Multimedia Press.

7
Science in the Early Years

Karen Hartley and Chris Macro

INTRODUCTION

It is generally accepted that science for young children involves them in situations where they are given the opportunity to engage with a variety of materials and events. Teachers encourage children to express ideas about what they notice and what they are doing so that they can develop the appropriate skills and understanding.

In this chapter we will identify the main challenges facing teachers in the early years classroom. During our work with teachers and students the following questions are those which are most commonly raised. We hope that our discussion will identify some strategies for consideration.

CHALLENGES

How much subject knowledge do I need to teach science effectively?

For much of the 1980s the message being transmitted to teachers in primary schools, particularly in early years classrooms, was that subject knowledge was less important than enthusiam and a willingness to learn alongside the children. The emphasis of the 1990s is somewhat different: indeed Carre and Bennett (1993) questioned whether teachers without relevant knowledge could provide appropriate experiences for children. Other writers, in an attempt to encourage the growth of primary science, stress that teachers with only limited background knowledge can and do teach primary science. The 'Three Wise Men' report suggests that 'good subject teaching depends upon the teachers' understanding of the subject concerned' (Alexander,

Rose and Woodhead, 1992). We feel that this statement should apply to knowledge of the content areas of science and also to knowledge about the learning and teaching of science. The part played by the processes and skills of science in children's learning must be recognised and developed whilst attitudes appropriate to science and the young child must be fostered. Teachers should use their understanding of how children learn and their knowledge of classroom management to present science in ways that are meaningful.

During a recent INSET course, teachers of nursery and infant children discussed the need for knowledge about science. Only a few considered themselves to have a science background but all shared the belief that the teacher had to show a genuine interest in science and in the children's ideas. There was agreement that lack of knowledge should not prevent a teacher from following a child's lead, nor instigating an investigation with a group of children. Similarly, they felt that some idea of the possible outcomes of science investigations was important. Many enquired about the different stages through which the understanding of a concept is developed in order to guide provision of relevant, logically sequenced experiences. They suggested that useful subject knowledge would include: how equipment and resources might be used; how materials would behave; what learning could be developed through specific activities.

As part of the INSET course, teachers kept a diary of observations of children involved in scientific experiences. These entries were shared and further development of the learning was discussed. Appropriate questions or other forms of intervention such as the use of analogies or explanations were suggested. Interestingly, whilst the teachers of the youngest children stated that they would probably intervene less often, or in a less direct manner, they felt they needed the same amount of scientific knowledge as their colleagues teaching children in Year 2. The opportunity for the teachers to work together on a range of tasks and activities emphasised the importance of talking through their understanding of a concept; for instance, the factors involved in whether an object floated. One headteacher commented that she intended to create opportunities for her staff to discuss their understanding of concepts, including matters such as progression and how key ideas within a concept might be different for a three-year-old and a seven-year-old.

For a teacher to admit to confusion, a degree of confidence and trust is required. Team planning and/or teaching could provide some opportunity for sharing ideas as could the identification of areas of science to be addressed during school-based INSET. Another way in which subject knowledge may be developed is through the use of schemes/published materials. These often include background information or an explanation of the concepts involved in the tasks suggested. Such knowledge of curricular materials available to support the teaching of science is said to be another kind of 'knowing about the subject' (Appendix 1 – useful addresses).

If we are to accept the current view that subject knowledge is important, how can it help us to become more effective in our teaching of science? We would suggest that knowledge about science should enable teachers to:

● provide appropriate experiences;

● develop key ideas;

● ask pertinent questions;

● encourage children to see links between experiences;

● give accurate explanations and use analogies that will be relevant to the child;

● help children make relevant observations when looking for evidence;

● know where to go next in terms of children's learning of a concept;

● reflect the role of science in society and everyday life.

Each of these is relevant to teaching in the early years but, perhaps above all, enhanced scientific understanding would bring greater confidence in developing science with young children.

How can we ensure that our provision for children in the early years is appropriate?

Following the revision of the National Curriculum, teachers have collaborated to evaluate schemes of work. Reflective teachers question whether this approach goes far enough and consider whether it might be appropriate to review teaching styles alongside pupils' experiences. They question whether all practical work provides pupils with learning opportunities and what criteria they could use to assess the potential of the experiences.

Various writers have expressed views about what constitutes effective practical work but there may be confusion about the terms used to describe aspects of practical work. Qualter et al (1990) suggest that exploration is 'much more than practical work' and involves the child in constructing new meaning from the experience. They suggest that exploration involves not only reflective problem-solving but also the practice of skills. Other writers may use the term 'investigation' to describe practical work which involves the development of skills as well as science ideas, whereas some teachers use the term 'experiment' to describe similar experiences. Since the requirements for Key Stage 1 state that pupils should 'use focused exploration and investigation to acquire scientific knowledge, understanding and skills' (DFE, 1995) it is important that teachers understand these terms. Our view is that *exploration* involves children using appropriate skills to interact with materials and may involve sharing observations about events. We understand *investigation* to be systematic enquiry where children plan and carry out tests to find the answer to a question. We feel that this distinction is important and that children should have the opportunity for both. Exploration has connotations of open-ended enquiry, whilst investigation is more constrained and follows set procedures. If learning is to take place as a result of practical science then the activity should provide opportunities for thinking. It is all too easy to be complacent about the idea that all 'hands on' experiences have intrinsic worth and will automatically result in learning.

In infant classrooms many teachers plan science experiences to develop observational skills but in reality these do not always achieve the intended outcome. Teachers need to be clear about the nature of observation in a scientific context. Feasey (1994) reported on research which showed that much of what teachers class as scientific observation 'turned out, in fact, to be art or language based'. For example, children engaged in observing plants and drawing them are doing art. It is only when they question why the plants display certain features that the activity becomes science.

The type of science-based experiences we would hope to find at Key Stage 1 are:

- practising particular skills; for example, using a timer to measure the time taken for a box to slide down a slope;

- making observations and using science ideas to make sense of what they notice; for example, when noticing that boxes covered with sandpaper do not slide down a slope and talking to the teacher about why they think this is happening;

- working on teacher-designed experiences in order to be exposed to a particular concept; for example, when sorting materials into those which are transparent, opaque or translucent;

- designing and carrying out a test in order to find an answer to a question which they or the teacher have posed; for example, when planning what to do to find which part of the classroom is the coolest.

Children at the end of Key Stage 1 will probably do all of these at some time during the school year but the contexts might be different for four and a half year olds. The youngest children will continue the exploration of their world which began as soon as they could put objects into their mouths. However, the touching, looking, feeling and tasting will be more focused and the teacher will provide opportunities for observing various phenomena which they will probably have encountered outside school. It is by channelling children's thoughts towards explanations, however tentative, that the teacher provides opportunities for scientific learning.

It is important to use contexts and skills with which the children are familiar and by way of illustration we will now look at an everyday example of a solid turning to a liquid with which children will be very familiar (see Figure 13). Thus we have an opportunity to move from everyday observation (early exploration) to scientific observation and investigation (guided and independent investigation).

The rate at which children move through the various stages will depend not only on their ability to visualise possible happenings but also on how often they have previously been given opportunities to work with the teacher in designing investigations. Although young children are often inquisitive they do need guidance in developing the scientific skills and they do need many opportunities to think and talk about ideas.

STRATEGIES

How important are the words? How can I get the children to think?

Earlier in this chapter reference was made to the way in which practical activities can develop children's thinking. When involved in practical work children might be engaged in a wide range of active processes, eg problem-solving, making sense of new experiences, making decisions. Thinking often involves use of logic, reason and, importantly, creativity; teachers need to develop these capacities in children. Adults

Experiences	*Possible learning*
Early exploration Children help the teacher to mix orange juice with water to make ice lollies by putting sticks into the tray and placing it in the freezer.	Teacher helps the children to notice how the liquid changes colour when water is added and how the sticks can move in the liquid. Children may observe that the liquid takes the shape of the container.
Lollies are taken out of the freezer. Children lick them and feel them.	Children are encouraged to talk about what they notice. The lollies are now hard and the stick is held firm by the frozen liquid (ice). As the children lick the lollies they feel cold and begin to soften. Some children may talk about the air or their warm mouths changing the shape and the texture of the ice.
One lolly is put back into a freezer bag. This is compared after a few minutes with those which are exposed to warm mouths.	Children may talk about what they notice. If a lolly is left in the freezer bag it stays hard and cold.
One lolly is left in the room on a saucer.	A lolly left in the room changes back to a liquid.
Guided investigation Teacher talks with and questions children about 'What will happen if we leave a lolly in the warm classroom?'	A lolly may melt in the warm classroom.
'What might happen if we leave a lolly in a fridge and another in a freezer bag?'	The lolly in the fridge may melt slowly. The lolly in the freezer bag will stay solid.
Teacher and children together plan a fair test to find out in what conditions the lollies melt: 1 lolly in a fridge, 1 lolly in a freezer bag, 1 lolly in a warm room. Teacher talks to children about how to keep the test fair:	Children are given opportunities to suggest what might happen (to predict). Children may recognise when a test is fair. Children talk about and try to give explanations about what they notice.

e.g. (a) same mixture of orange and water
(b) same size and shape of lolly
(c) when lollies are frozen hard leave them in the fridge, freezer bag and room for the same length of time. Observe and discuss results.

Present results by drawing, writing or using teacher-designed tables.

Independent investigation

Children look at lollies of different shapes, and are encouraged to raise questions, eg does a short, wide lolly melt more quickly than a long, thin lolly?

Turning ideas into a form which can be investigated. Thinking about what might happen, eg 'I think a long, thin lolly will melt more quickly than a short, wide lolly.'

Children plan what to do in order to answer the question, eg What might they use as jelly moulds? How long to leave in the freezer? What variables should they keep the same (eg same amount of liquid)?

Planning what to do. Making measurements. Children measure liquids and record time left in the freezer, fridge and room.

How to decide which melts most quickly?

Recording observations by writing and drawing; for example, after 3, 5 and 10 minutes. Using results to draw conclusions. Providing explanations.

Fig. 13. From early exploration to guided and independent investigation

can extend children's thinking by responding appropriately to their questions and comments. They may encourage the children to observe carefully, recognise patterns and identify similarities and differences and use these observations to develop children's ideas about scientific phenomena. Enabling children to link one experience to another, by reminding them of related events or pointing out the relationship, will deepen their understanding of a concept.

Teachers' questions which may be effective in encouraging thinking will be those used to elicit and challenge currently held ideas, to instigate problem-solving and to ask children for explanations and reasons as to why things happen or are as they are. In science children need to have practical experience of abstract ideas and should test their own ideas in order to confirm or reject these. As children offer explanations they have the opportunity to reorganise and clarify their thoughts. HMI (1989) considered that discussion where children are encouraged to predict, plan, reflect and explain is a 'crucial element of effective science teaching.'

Giving children time to think before expecting an answer to a complex question gives value to the thinking process. Teachers need to wait for children to formulate their thoughts; often when children are given time to do this their answers indicate a high level of thinking.

'Can there be thought without words?' Fisher (1990) suggests there is and considers the importance of visual thinking in children's learning. However, teachers are concerned about children's language development and recognise the use of language in developing under-standing. Children are often asked to demonstrate their knowledge through language. What form should this language take? Many teachers are unsure as to the importance that should be attached to the use of scientific vocabulary and are not sure whether this indicates greater knowledge or understanding. Research shows that this is not necessarily the case (SPACE, 1989). It would seem that children must first be comfortable with describing or explaining their thoughts in everyday language. Scientific vocabulary should be introduced in context and the use of analogies and metaphors may help children link the experience with the 'label' (Sherrington, 1993). The class teacher, who knows the children and their facility with language, is the best person to judge when to introduce appropriate vocabulary.

How do I know they're learning through play?

Perhaps the initial response to this question should echo Janet Atkin (1991) when she suggests that it is more appropriate to consider what is *not* being learned through children's play. We need to recognise that there is no straightforward answer to the question and that much will depend upon a teacher's perceptions of 'play'.

There is a wealth of literature (Moyles, 1994 and Bruce, 1992 amongst others) as to what constitutes play and it indicates that play is an opportunity for children to experiment and try out their ideas in a non-threatening situation. It allows children to repeat, manipulate and practise skills and experiences.

Another claim for the value of play, particularly when self-initiated, is that it can motivate children's learning as individuals and in co-operation with others. One aspect of the teacher's role, therefore, is to provide opportunities which enable children to start with what they know, make links between experiences, reflect on them and talk about them with their peers. An early years teacher who offers an exciting, stimulating environment can provide many opportunities for quality learning whereby children can develop their scientific awareness through play.

Perhaps a feature within the teacher's weekly or daily plan would be to allocate time during the school day to join in, support and extend children's play particularly in those areas where the potential for scientific exploration/investigation is most easily recognised. These would include activities in the sand, water and construction areas but there will, in addition, be other activities which could be utilised to develop children's thinking. For example, in a role play area which is set up as a hospital, children could 'explore' external and internal parts of the body through the use of X-rays involved in play.

Teachers may feel unsure as to how to intervene in children's play. We suggest that the strategies employed will be those that are consistently recognised as essential techniques in effective teaching: wondering, explaining, suggesting, questioning, demonstrating, reviewing, challenging, even instructing! At the same time, though, children should be allowed and encouraged to take the lead in using all or any of these strategies with the teacher during the play.

An education student researched the potential and actual learning in a free-flow play situation by observing young children's actions with both dry and damp sand. She made notes of her observations and from these she identified aspects that indicated thinking of a scientific nature and was able to gather evidence about individual children's learning. She recognised that early ideas about change in, properties of, and the use of materials can be encouraged as can scientific processes. If teachers identify the learning in play and plan accordingly then the findings of Ofsted (1993) that 'Fewer than half the teachers (of Reception classes) fully exploited the educational potential of play' could be reversed.

How can I encourage collaborative work with young children?

Teachers of young children who have learned to work co-operatively may wish to encourage their pupils to develop these skills and encourage their children to work collaboratively. Research into this area is reported in Galton and Williamson (1992) and here co-operative group work is defined as that which requires children to work on different tasks in order to produce a joint outcome. An example of this might be where a group of children worked together to produce a book about the weather and each child wrote a separate page. The group then shared their work with the rest of the class.

Whilst this type of work has value, it does not necessarily encourage children to talk together and to listen to each other. True collaborative work involves children sharing jobs and making decisions together in order to complete a task which appeals to them. When working collaboratively, less confident children can be enthused by others. As the aim is to develop thinking through communication, this type of work can be useful, not only in developing concepts, but also in allowing children to practise skills. For example, when children talk together to decide which is the 'best' from a selection of balls, they must agree on what they mean by best and then work out a strategy to solve the problem. This procedure will develop planning and investigative skills as well as social and linguistic skills.

Children who spend most of their time sitting in groups but working individually will need to be introduced gradually to collaborative work. Berry and Walker (1989) observed that seven-year-old children generally worked 'alongside rather than together . . . in the group rather than with the group'. However, the writers were positive and optimistic about the value of collaborative work and described how one group of girls was able to involve all group members in the same task.

Planning and carrying out science investigations in small groups can be a useful context for developing collaborative skills and there are some Key Stage 1 children who do this regularly. Those who are successful are usually from schools where children are involved in decision-making and everyone's ideas are valued.

Some teachers begin collaborative work by asking children to work in pairs on a fairly structured task such as sorting materials into sets or deciding what work is done by a machine shown in a picture. The pairs then meet another pair and the ideas are shared again. Children are encouraged to look at each other when they are talking and to take turns to speak. Occasionally some teachers use an artefact such as a wooden spoon which children hold when they speak. This may prevent everyone talking at once!

Other strategies which teachers have used in order to keep children's minds on the task are:

- to teach them how to proceed if there are arguments;

- to encourage them to evaluate their work and to talk about how effective they have been at turn-taking and listening to each other;

- to discuss how children feel if their ideas are dismissed or mocked;

- to suggest that they have a group leader who asks children in turn to give their ideas.

Horbury and Pears (1994) observed six- and seven-year-olds whilst they were engaged in collaborative work and found that after a period of time children were able to 'deal effectively with any tensions and conflict which arose.'

Certainly those teachers who regularly provide situations where children work together on the same problem have been pleased at the high level of motivation in their pupils.

What are the important stages in planning science for young children?

Consider as a typical example the hypothetical case of Mrs Smith teaching a combined Reception and Year 1 class and who is preparing her medium-term plans for a five-week period. She notes from the school's long-term plans that the concepts she has to address focus on light and colour. She is also aware that the school's science policy states that there should be a strong emphasis on developing investigative skills.

Step 1

Using the appropriate Programmes of Study and Nursery Desirable Outcomes (SCAA, 1996), guidelines she identifies the key ideas that she hopes most of the children will learn about sources of light and how light behaves.

Step 2

She then looks at the assessment notes which she and another teacher have made about the children. These show that six children from the Year 1 group understand the concept of a fair test and with help can interpret simple forms of recording. Other children in the Year 1 group are less confident in recognising a fair test. Robert, who has special educational needs, enjoys practical work, can describe orally what he notices but needs a great deal of support.

Step 3

She refers to her notes about the Reception children in a similar way and begins her medium-term planning where the experiences are identified. She takes account of the school's scheme of work so that she is aware of what experiences children will encounter in future years. She now knows the needs of the children and what skills and ideas should be developed.

Step 4
When planning for the week she considers the adult help available, which experiences will be ongoing and part of the interactive display, and which activities are appropriate for the different groups of children.

Mrs Smith uses a combination of whole-class teaching, groupwork and play to develop children's learning. She makes a careful note of children's achievements and their experiences and shares these with colleagues at the end of the school year.

EVALUATION

In our discussion we have drawn, not only on our experiences, but also on the evidence from research into young children's learning. We hope that the questions we have raised will stimulate teachers to come together to address the challenges of developing science with children in the early years. To be confident about their success in meeting these challenges they will need to review the extent to which:

- their personal knowledge of key ideas in and about science has been developed;

- they have considered ways in which children can work collaboratively;

- they have identified the learning potential of children's play;

- they recognise the different types of practical work and the part these play in children's learning;

- they are aware of the importance of encouraging children to think and express ideas and to allow for this in their planning.

USEFUL READING

There are many publications intended to develop teachers' knowledge and understanding. Amongst these are:

Archer, D. (1991) *What's your reaction*? Royal Society of Chemistry.

Nuffield Primary Science (1993–96) *Teachers' Resource Material.* Collins Educational.

NCC/SCAA (1992–94) *Knowledge and Understanding of Science: teachers' Guides.*

Teachers' materials to accompany schools' broadcasts are also a useful source of background information.

BIBLIOGRAPHY

Alexander, R., Rose, J. and Woodhead, C. (1992) *Curriculum Organisation and Classroom Practice in Primary Schools.* London: DES.

Atkin, J. (1991) Thinking About Play, in N. Hall and L. Abbott (eds) *Play in the National Curriculum.* London: Hodder and Stoughton.

Berry, T. and Walker, U. (1989) Assessing Children's Collaborative Skills by Paired Observation. *Education 3–13*, vol. 17, no. 3, pp. 18–24.

Birchall, L. (1993) Sand: An Educational Resource. Unpublished Dissertation.

Black, P. and Harlen, W. (Directors) (1989) Science Processes and Concept Exploration Reports. Liverpool: Liverpool University Press

Bruce, T. (1992) *Time To Play in Early Childhood Education.* London: Hodder and Stoughton.

Carre, C. and Bennett, N. (1993) Subject Matter Matters Primary Science Review, no. 29, pp. 11–13

DFE (1995) *Science in the National Curriculum.* London: HMSO.

Feasey, R. (1994) *The Challenge of Science,* in Aubrey (ed.) *The Role of Subject Knowledge in the Early Years of Schooling.* London: Falmer Press.

Fisher, R. (1990) *Teaching Children to Think.* Oxford: Blackwell Education.

Galton, M. and Williamson, J. (1992) *Group Work in the Primary School.* London: Routledge.

HMI (1989) *Aspects of Primary Teaching – The Teaching and Learning of Science.* London: HMSO.

Horbury, A. and Pears, H. (1994) Collaborative Group Work: How Infant Children Can Manage It. *Education 3–13*, vol. 22, no. 3, pp. 20–28.

Moyles, J. (ed.) (1994) *Excellence of Play.* Milton Keynes: Open University Press.

Ofsted (1993) *First Class.* London: HMSO.

Qualter, A. et al (1990) *Exploration: A Way of Learning Science.* Oxford: Blackwell.

Sherrington, R. (ed.) (1993) *Primary Science Teachers' Handbook.* London: Simon Schuster/ASE.

8
Science 1

David Byrne

CONTEXT

Science 1: How did it get there?

The National Curriculum for Science was introduced into maintained schools in England and Wales in September 1989 and was designed to provide a broad and balanced range of scientific ideas and skills and contexts through which teachers could structure a science curriculum appropriate to the 5–16 age range. The orders comprised two types of understanding, namely conceptual understanding, in which scientific knowledge was drawn together, and procedural understanding, in which scientific skills and processes were developed. When the orders were introduced to the 5–11 sector, they caused great consternation amongst teachers, the major concern of primary teachers being related to Attainment Target 1 (Science 1). The emphasis at both Key Stage 1 and Key Stage 2 was upon children being active. Although most primary teachers were not strangers to this approach to learning, especially at Key Stage 1, Attainment Target 1 confused and threatened their security. They were unsure about the meaning and relevance of such words as 'hypothesis' and 'variable' and did not know how these related to the primary classroom or what relevance such terms had for primary children. One could be forgiven for thinking that little or no consultation with the primary sector had been carried out. The terminology used in the orders was unfriendly and alienated many excellent teachers.

In 1992 a revision of the orders was completed by the National Curriculum Council. It altered much of this terminology as well as changing its presentation, but retained for Science 1 the emphasis upon activity. Primary teachers continued to persevere with their efforts to put into practice the programmes of study associated with this attainment target but still found many aspects of it difficult to implement fully. For example, allowing pupils the freedom to make their own decisions and plan their own investigations often created noise and disruption in the classroom. The support in terms of INSET by local authorities was being constantly eroded by other pressures within the system and problems remained.

In 1993 the Dearing review of the National Curriculum produced yet another revision of the Science orders. Science 1 was renamed Experimental and Investigative Science but still retained its dominant position as part of a balanced science curriculum in primary schools.

Why teach children process skills?

There had been considerable debate for some years about the balance that should be struck between children acquiring scientific knowledge and scientific skills. The National Curriculum faced this dilemma head on when it included Science 1 as part of the original 1989 orders and maintained it throughout the revisions. Justification for its inclusion can be made by looking at research into the way in which pupils learn in science. Harlen (1992) argues that, 'The development of understanding in science is . . . dependent on the ability to carry out process skills in a scientific manner.' She is claiming that in order for children to develop scientific ideas they need also to develop the process skills of science. She believes that without these skills their ideas will be 'based on casual observation, non-investigated events and the acceptance of hearsay, [and] are likely to be non-scientific, "everyday" ideas' (1985). In other words, they will develop ideas to explain their world whether or not school teaches science. One of the implications of this is that if school does not help children to grasp the right ideas then children will develop misconceptions which may be difficult to change, as McGuigan and Schilling point out in Chapter 2.

Science 1 ensures that a child interacts with the environment. They can touch or feel or observe events and then test out their own ideas. It is not enough simply to tell a child something. Research (Osborne and Freyberg, 1985) indicates that ownership is an effective way of ensuring meaningful learning. Meaningful learning is a theory developed by Ausubel (1968). It partially embraces the learning theories of Piaget (1966) in that it values the need for children to experience concrete learning in order to achieve abstract thought. Ausubel and Piaget differ from each other, however, in that Ausubel argues that a child needs to be able to verbalise their thoughts in order to develop concepts. The school of thought which promotes these beliefs is called constructivism. McGuigan and Schilling discuss this more fully in Chapter 2. Constructivism suggests that children make their own interpretations of information that they receive through their senses. Science 1 enables this to occur. It is vital in order for a child to reject an idea that they may hold, that they have their existing ideas challenged. Driver and Bell (1985) summarise the main points of constructivism by arguing that a number of points need to be considered if children are to become effective learners. These points may be summarised thus:

- It is important to value the ideas that a child brings to their science lessons from their everyday experiences. A child's head is not empty!

- Learning takes place as a result of an interaction between the child's physical and social environment. Such experiences enable a child to move on from current ideas to new ones.

- Children are constantly checking their existing ideas. They need to restructure these in order to move on in their thinking.

- No matter what a teacher does, the child will believe or reject an idea introduced to him or her.

- Learning is essentially an active process and must involve the child.

Science 1, Experimental and Investigative Science, offers teachers the opportunity to involve pupils, use their senses and thereby challenge previously held views. Science 1 is totally interlinked with the knowledge Attainment Targets 2, 3 and 4. The concepts to be developed in the areas of knowledge give purpose to the activities related to Science 1 whilst enabling children to take ownership of their learning and thereby heighten their chances of restructuring and accepting new scientific ideas and concepts. Children need skill as well as knowledge. Wynne Harlen (1993) identifies six skills that are relevant to primary age children:

- observing
- hypothesising
- predicting
- investigating

- drawing conclusions

- communicating.

These skills are seen as contributing to the physical and mental activities required for a child to develop ideas about the world around them. The National Curriculum (DES, 1995) broadly reflects these skills although they are not presented in the same way.

CHALLENGES

The programme of study for Science 1 at both Key Stages 1 and 2 are divided into three sections:

- planning experimental work;

- obtaining evidence;

- considering evidence.

These three sections need to be interpreted.

Planning experimental work
Pupils are expected to develop increasingly independent skills related to planning. In order to do this they need to be able to take an idea, often in the form of a prediction, and plan the steps required to prove or disprove it. This involves:

- identifying what information needs to be collected;

- selecting appropriate equipment to be used;

- carrying out a fair test or observing accurately according to the type of activity being carried out;

- preparing appropriate models for pupils to record the outcomes.

Obtaining evidence
Pupils are expected to be able to transfer their plans into actions. They will need to show an ability to use equipment appropriately and accurately in order to gather information. This may involve using standard units accurately related to temperature, distance, time, force, weight or volume, or it may simply demand accurate observations with the naked eye or with the help of a hand lens or microscope.

Considering evidence

Pupils need to be able to record the information gathered in a way which can be understood by others. They may use a variety of ways of recording methods depending upon the type of activity being carried out. Examples include completing prompt sheets, using script to record sequences of events, completing tables, charts or graphs, creating diagrams and drawings or creating labelled models. One should not discount the creative and expressive forms of communication; for example, encouraging pupils to demonstrate principles and ideas through drama.

The crucial point is that the recording should meet the learning objectives of the activity and be appropriate to the child's needs. The child should be able to use the information gathered in order to reflect and evaluate upon what they have done.

These three sections jointly contribute to developing children's ability to experiment and investigate. The emphasis is upon practical learning, but what is practical work all about?

Science 1 is practical, but what is practical science?

When the National Curriculum was first introduced, primary teachers were told to step up the amount of practical work in science. My experience of teaching in many classrooms, as well as delivering INSET for primary teachers throughout the north west, indicates that the nature and range of practical work that occurred often missed out on the needs of children. It seemed that activity for activity's sake was often the order of the day. Even now many teachers feel under pressure always to follow a more open-ended, whole-investigation approach rather than providing a balance of practical work. Experienced teachers have, however, now begun to question the value of offering practical work without the structural support required to enable children to solve investigations. A view has gathered pace that a child cannot apply skills which have not been learnt!

The Dearing review (1993) has to a large extent reflected such concerns. The pendulum has now started to swing back to balance. Practical work is still valued but there is a clearer understanding of the range of methods that this might entail. An open-ended, investigative approach is still important, indeed it remains the ultimate target for a child to achieve, but there is not recognition of the need to build children's abilities up through a number of approaches. The now superseded National Curriculum Council document (NCC, 1993), suggested that there are four types of practical activity that are relevant to primary science. These remain important today and relate to activities which involve the development of:

Observation skills

If a child cannot observe accurately and use their senses to gather information, that child's ability to act scientifically will be limited. The earliest experiences at school should encourage observational work of all types, and skills should be developed as they move through the system. It is only from applying the results of observation that a child can begin to see patterns and make predictions leading to the need to test out their ideas. Observations enable a child to question their existing views and begin to restructure what they believe.

Basic skills

These give children confidence and the ability to use equipment effectively in order to collect information. With younger children it may be as simple as using a ruler properly or weighing an object using a balance with non-standard weights. An older child may use a thermometer to measure and record the temperature of water or collect information about changing light intensity with a suitable computer-linked sensor. Without a range of basic skills a child is severely restricted in their ability to carry out either experiments or investigations.

Experimental skills

The term 'experiment' often instils fear into the hearts of primary teachers. It can bring back memories of poor experiences of science at secondary school when science seemed to be simply a case of doing tedious, teacher-directed activities and then writing up what they had done using the rigid format of Apparatus, Method and Conclusion. This need not be the case, however, and what is termed an experimental approach has its place in science at primary school as long as it is part of a range of practical activities. Experiments provide a child with a valuable dimension to their science work.

Investigative skills

It can be argued that the four types of practical work form a hierarchy. A child needs to be able to use simple and basic equipment appropriately and accurately. These skills can then be applied to carrying out experiments. An experiment involves children performing tasks which are presented to them in a controlled and restricted style. It has clear objectives supported by a structured approach and the teacher has a clear expectation of the outcome. An experiment can often be used to illustrate scientific ideas.

An investigation, on the other hand, demands that a child makes decisions which are increasingly independent of an adult. They take on a problem or identify a prediction and then go on to plan, carry out and draw conclusions from the information collected in order to find out. For children to be able to carry out an investigation effectively they need to be able to observe accurately, apply basic skills and transfer the training received in carrying out an experiment to a new, more open-ended situation. The implications for classroom teaching are, of course, enormous.

What does the jargon mean?

The role of the class teacher is vital when developing scientific processes in the classroom. There must be an adequate understanding by the teacher of the main stages of the scientific process. Questions which are frequently asked are discussed below.

What is a prediction and an hypothesis?

A child makes a prediction by saying what he/she thinks will happen. The word 'guess' is sometimes associated with a prediction. An hypothesis is made whenever he/she gives a possible reason for that prediction. For example, a child may say, 'I think that the car will go further along the carpet, because the carpet is smoother.' If the child makes this statement then the child can be encouraged to do a test.

What is fair testing all about?

Whether you are working with six-year-olds or eleven-year-olds, the National Curriculum demands that children begin to develop skills related to fair testing. At Key Stage 1 a child should be able to explain the basic idea, but by the end of Key Stage 2 a child needs to have the confidence and ability actually to carry out a simple, relevant and appropriate test independently and in so doing demonstrate an understanding of the meaning of fair testing in practice. Fair testing involves being able to handle variables. The difficulty here is understanding the meaning of the term 'variable'. A variable can be defined as a quantity that can take different values. Children need to be able to recognise and handle three types of variable with reasonable independence by the age of eleven. By identifying them separately they can be more easily understood:

- **The independent variable**. This is the one factor that should be changed in an investigation. For example, a child may be investigating toy cars in order to find the 'best surface'. In order to do this they will need to change the surface that they are testing. This is the independent variable. Children can refer to it as 'the thing that needs to be changed'.

- **The dependent variable.** This refers to the measurement or information that is to be collected in order to test out the prediction. In the example above the dependent variable will be the measurement of the distance travelled by the toy vehicles. Children can refer to this as 'the things that have to be measured'.

- **The control variable/s.** In an investigation, most aspects of the investigation must remain constant so that the measurements are not affected by anything other than the thing that is being tested, ie the independent variable. For the example, factors such as the height of the slope, the toy itself, the starting position, etc must remain the same in each test. Many children will automatically recognise this but not consistently. It is vital that children are constantly exposed to an expectation to carry out 'fair testing' as they move through the school. Children will need to consider 'what must remain the same?'

How can children record?

Recording is an integral part of Science 1 but can become a burden to both child and teacher if thought is not given to it. It can be the most important part of science at primary school because it offers a chance for a child to be reflective and yet it is so often marginalised because of lack of time. Some schools include science recording as part of their maths or English work thereby extending the time available as well as adding relevance to the other curriculum areas. The role of the teacher is vital here (see below, Making it work in the classroom). Creative planning can promote exciting recording. It is essential that children are given the opportunity to report their experiments and investigations as well as representing results in a variety of ways. Carre and Ovens (1994) identify a number of ways in which children can write about science. Examples that they include are:

- **Small step writing**. This is a way of building up a child's ability to write a full report. They suggest that before the investigation a child may be asked to plan what they are going to do. Prompt sheets may be introduced at this stage (see below, Making it work in the classroom). During the actual investigation itself, ask them to make notes in a rough book or fill in a table or label a prepared diagram. After the investigation, a child may be asked to complete another prompt sheet (see below, Making it work in the class-room). They may write down suggestions as to why their results differ from others' or be asked to draw the events that they have observed including appropriate captions.

- **Writing to understand the science which has been done**. Carre and Ovens (1994) offer a variety of alternative ideas for children's writing in science. Their suggestions include:
(a) Write a newspaper article based upon the information collected in an experiment.
(b) Rewrite a small part of a textbook.
(c) Describe what it must be like to be inside a plant or an animal, eg a journey of a platelet around the blood system.
(d) Ask for a set of instructions for an investigation to be written up for use by a younger child (perhaps for an identified younger child as part of a class/pupil exchange within a primary school).
(e) Prepare reports for use via electronic mail.

- **Using tables, charts and graphs.** It is important that from the youngest of ages children are given the opportunity to develop skills related to presentation of results. During Key Stage 1 a child may begin to record collected measurements on a prepared table. This information may then be transferred to a simple block graph which is constructed with the teacher's help. More able children will begin to do this without too much support if they are given sufficient practice. By the age of eleven a child should be able to construct their own tables and be able to make a variety of graphs to represent the results, including bar charts, block graphs and pie charts.

What is the meaning of evaluation?

As a result of the information collected as part of a practical investigation or an experiment, a child needs to be encouraged to look for patterns in their observations or measurements. They need to be able to make links between their prediction and the outcome of their tests. Was the prediction correct? If it wasn't, are there any possible reasons for this? Would it be possible to alter the way that the test was done so that the information gathered would be more accurate or reliable? Many children find this difficult to do but with practice and encouragement it can come with maturity.

STRATEGIES

Making it work in the classroom

The role of the teacher is vital in enabling a child to become competent in Science 1. The methodology adopted within the class and the overall expectations in day-to-day teaching both within the class as well as across the school are factors influencing the child's scientific development. If a child is encouraged to act with independence in their school life then the demands of Science 1 will be met much more easily. A child who can take out their own books and pencils, who is expected to organise their own table and take responsibility for an aspect of class organisation is much more likely to cope with Science 1. Ultimately a child needs to be able to make decisions and stand by them. There are many strategies to achieve this that one can adopt. The most important are discussed here.

Careful planning

In an attempt to ensure that all aspects of the knowledge attainment targets are delivered, it is easy to plan for content at the expense of processes. One should ensure that there are planned learning outcomes not only for the programmes of study for Science 2, 3 and 4 but also relevant outcomes associated with Science 1. The skills that one plans should link into the activities planned for the knowledge.

- Example 1. You may plan to develop a child's concept of friction and force by testing cars moving across different surfaces. This activity would enable you to plan learning outcomes related to predicting, fair testing and recording with graphs.

- Example 2. The content focus may be changed as a result of energy transfer caused by heating. A child could explore the way in which ice melts. The skills that may be planned alongside this could be related to the basic skills of using a thermometer correctly and recording temperature change over a period of time.

Across an academic year, care should be taken to ensure that a child is given a range of opportunities to develop the processes and skills identified by the National Curriculum. Whole key stage planning can ensure that progression and continuity in the delivery of scientific processes can occur.

Class organisation

Getting the organisation right is very important. It is naive to attempt to identify a particular model of class organisation. Many factors influence this. Before organising your class, ask yourself the following questions:

- How many children do I have?

- How big is the class area and associated activity areas?

- What type of practical work will I be using? Will it be observation, basic skills teaching, experimental work or investigative work? The latter two usually demand more space and resources which can influence the organisation of the class.

- What resources do I need to achieve my aims?

- Will extra adults be available, eg NNEB, parent helper, colleague, work experience person?

- Are there any children with special needs within the class?

When these answers are established, decisions about possible organisation can be made. Options include:

- Whole class introduction in which key questions are raised, predictions made and purposes of activities clarified, followed up by the class working in groups on the same activities at the same time or in groups working at different times throughout the day or week.

- Activities carried out by small groups at different times of the day or week directly supported by an adult helper.

- A demonstration to the whole class with children completing written/graphic tasks based upon it.

- Groups or individuals being given the opportunity to plan, research and find answers to questions that with help and guidance they have phrased themselves. This is your ultimate target!

Be flexible, no two classes or groups of children are the same!

Teacher intervention

The contact between yourself and the child is crucial. The level of intervention can alter the outcomes of a child's learning activity dramatically. The range of possible interventions can be summarised thus:

- *Directing.* You demonstrate or tell a child what to do.

- *Guiding.* You encourage a child towards a certain action or direction.

- *Questioning.* You intervene with a question which moves a child forward in their learning and encourages a response. For example:
  (a) Can you tell me what you can see?
  (b) Which is the fastest/smallest/heaviest?
  (c) What will happen if?
  (d) Can you find a way to . . . ?
  The type of question asked is often linked to the learning outcome you have planned for Science 1.

- *Differentiating.* This is often linked to questions you ask. A more able child can be asked to carry out a more advanced question than a less able. For example, a more able child could be asked to measure the speed of toy car involving measuring time and distance whilst a less able child may be asked to simply observe the one that goes the fastest. Stuart Naylor and Brenda Keogh say more about this in Chapter 5.

Promoting children's independence through guiding planning, recording and evaluating skills

Prompt sheets have proved to be an effective classroom tool for structuring practical work in science, especially more open-ended activities. An investigation can be divided into the three stages outlined in the National Curriculum Programmes of Study. For each stage it is possible to devise a prompt sheet which offers the chance for children to be guided or for them to act independently of the teacher. Examples of possible sheets are set out in Figures 14 and 15.

It is possible to be as creative or as formal as you wish in the design of such sheets. The sheets I have designed as an example are in the shape of a parachute. They can be related to any topic being studied. In this case it might be flight. The three sheets can be turned into an investigation book with a cover and a back. The book could include drawings, photographs or CD ROM images. There is much scope for links with English, art, and design technology.

- *Sheet 1.* (Figure 14.) This sheet is to guide children at the early

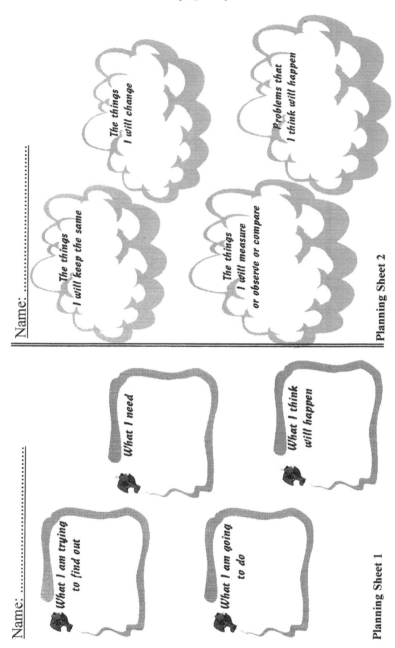

Name: ....

The things
I will keep the same

The things
I will change

The things
I will measure
or observe or compare

Problems that
I think will happen

Planning Sheet 2

Name: ....

What I am trying
to find out

What I need

What I am going
to do

What I think
will happen

Planning Sheet 1

My Results Sheet

Name:..........................

1. These are my results:

2. This is why I think these results happened:

3. These are the problems I met:

4. If I repeated this activity, I would change:

Fig. 15.   Results sheets

stages of planning. They are asked to say what they are trying to find out, decide what they will need, plan what they are going to do and make a prediction of what they think might happen.

You may want to encourage the idea of fair testing and you could introduce this idea by asking three key questions:

What are you going to measure?

What are you going to keep the same?

What do you need to change?

- *Sheet 2.* (Figure 14.) Children with more experience of planning may use this sheet together with the first. They will have to consider the three key questions when completing their planning sheet.

- *Sheet 3.* (Figure 15.) This guides children by asking them to record their final measurements, comparisons and observations. It is important that they consider why they had the results that they did, if they are to begin to link their practical investigation to the development of their scientific understanding.

EVALUATION

After the hurly burly of the practical work, stop and give children time to think about whether their predictions were correct. What did they find out? Are there more activities they could do or questions they could answer? Did they enjoy it? This stage is perhaps more valuable than any other but it can easily be overlooked. Make sure that time is built into the planning in order to ensure that children have time to reflect!

BIBLIOGRAPHY

Ausubel, D. (1968) *Educational Psychology.* New York: Holt Rinehart and Winston.

Carre, C. and Ovens, C. (1994) *Science 7–11: Developing Primary Teaching Skills.* London: Routledge.

Dearing, R. (1993) *The National Curriculum and its Assessment.* London: School Curriculum and Assessment Authority.

Department for Education (1995) *Science in the National Curriculum.* London: HMSO.

Driver, R. and Bell, B. (1985) Students' Thinking and the Learning of Science: A Constructivist View. *School Science Review*, March 1986, pp. 443–56.

Harlen, W. (1985) *Primary Science: Taking the Plunge.* London: Heinemann.

Harlen, W. (1992) *The Teaching of Science.* London: David Fulton.

Harlen, W. (1993) *Teaching and Learning Primary Science.* London: Heinemann.

NCC (1993) *Teaching Science at K.S. 1 and 2.* York: NCC.

Ollerenshaw, C. and Ritchie, R. (1993) *Primary Science: Making it Work.* London: David Fulton.

Open University (1991) *Science for Primary Teachers.* Milton Keynes: Open University Press.

Osborne, R. and Freyberg, P. (1985) *Learning in Science.* Auckland, New Zealand: Heinemann.

Piaget, J. (1966) *The Growth of Logical Thinking.* London: Routledge & Keegan Paul.

Qualter, A. et al (1990) *Exploration: a Way of Learning.* Oxford: Blackwell.

Whitelegg, E., Thomas, J. and Tresman, S. (1993) *Challenges and Opportunities for Science Education.* London: Paul Chapman Publishing/Open University.

9
Assessment and Recording as a Constructive Process

Ron Ritchie

INTRODUCTION

The main focus of this chapter is the notion that assessment is essential to effective teaching: without assessing children, teachers cannot make the professional judgements necessary to decide on appropriate interventions, or the next steps for learners. The chapter argues that assessment is a constructive process for teachers, which has parallels with the ways in which children learn. When learning, children are constructing their own unique understanding of the world around them through engagement with that world. With assessment the teacher is actively constructing a unique understanding of individual learners' skills and scientific understanding through interaction with them.

This chapter explores the practical implications of making such an approach work in a busy classroom. We begin by clarifying the nature of assessment in science, and the relationship between the approach to assessment introduced here and the statutory assessment requirements of the National Curriculum in England and Wales. In the past, assessment has often been confused with the recording of children's achievements: in this chapter the relationship between the separate elements – assessment, recording and reporting – is explored. The national Curriculum for Science focuses on skills, processes and knowledge and understanding. The implications for assessing these dimensions are discussed, with a reminder that there is more to science education than the National Curriculum. The chapter then explores the role of the teacher and offers specific examples of teaching strategies to support assessment. The National Curriculum

122

requirements are revisited before a section which highlights issues related to recording and reporting. The final section relates assessment and evaluation, within the framework of the reflective practitioner.

THE CHALLENGE

The nature and purposes of assessment

The introduction of the National Curriculum for Science and the emphasis in government pronouncements and the media on statutory assessment requirements have clouded many teachers' perceptions of the nature of assessment and its purposes. Various Secretaries of State for Education have fostered the view that assessment is solely concerned with making summative judgements about pupils' achievements, usually suggesting that the simplest way to do this is using paper and pencil tests. The purpose of assessment in the eyes of these politicians is to ensure the accountability of schools, rather than to facilitate learning. This, together with the pre-Dearing overcrowded curriculum and the complexity caused by assessment of too many statements of attainment and unrealistic expectations about recording children's achievements, deflected attention from other aspects of assessment. The 'slimmed down' curriculum (DFE, 1995), more realistic statutory assessment requirements and a five-year period for consolidation offer the scope for us to re-emphasise the nature and value of formative teacher assessment. This will allow teachers to focus on assessment as essential to teaching: assessment as the means by which a teacher gains insights into children's learning.

Formative assessment is used to inform decisions about what to do next to further a child's learning. This formative purpose is the one emphasised in this chapter. Assessments of children are one of the ways in which teachers evaluate the success or otherwise of their teaching. Both of these purposes can be met through ongoing classroom assessments that are integral to everyday teaching; they do not necessarily require special tests or activities. However, they do require teachers to note or collect evidence of children's learning and make informed judgements about it. This evidence can be concerned with what children do, what they produce or what they say. To identify such evidence teachers must listen actively to what children say, they must ask focused questions based on children's responses and must be alert to the unexpected. The hardest part for the teacher is recognising significance in the mass of evidence available to them every time they work with children.

There is an important link between assessment, progression and differentiation. For children's learning to be progressive, teachers need to address individual needs by differentiating tasks and interventions (Russell et al 1994). All children do not learn in the same way: it is not possible to prescribe a series of specific steps towards higher understanding (although more general statements can usefully be made). The only way to ensure a child moves towards more sophisticated understanding is for the teacher to plan the next step, based on her/his understanding of the child' current understanding, and on the teacher's understanding of the science concept involved. The teacher is engaging in a constructive process: seeking to build up as accurate a picture as possible of the child's current understanding, mapping that against her/his understanding of the science concept involved and then identifying a way forward.

The approach to assessment advocated in this chapter matches well the approach to teaching, based on a constructivist view of learning, which was outlined earlier in the book. The phases of such an approach – orientation, elicitation, intervention, reviewing and application – can all offer opportunities for assessment (see Ollerenshaw and Ritchie, 1997). In particular, elicitation, as a means of children clarifying their existing ideas and teachers gaining access to such ideas, is essentially a form of assessment. Few primary teachers would argue with the idea of 'starting from where the children are'. To do this requires a teacher to put considerable effort into finding out where that starting point lies. However, that is only the first part of the story; the decisions based on such insights present a problem. Children's learning is undoubtedly a complex process and one decision about an appropriate intervention is unlikely to be enough. Assessment has to be ongoing and all-embracing. As the children move from exploration into investigations, through to reviewing and applying new ideas in other situations, the teacher needs to remain alert for significant evidence of learning (or indeed, blocks to learning).

In contrast to the above, the summative purpose of assessment (emphasised through the National Curriculum statutory requirements) is intended to identify a child's achievements at the end of a unit of work or at a particular stage of a child's school life. Summative assessment is important and can make a significant contribution to teachers' evaluation of their work as well as to the education of individual learners, as long as it is valid – providing a genuine indication of children's achievements. Within the National Curriculum, teachers are required to carry out summative assessments to ascribe a child to a level, using the specified Level Descriptions, at the end of each Key Stage. These results are reported to parents (alongside the results of the standardised assessment tasks and tests – SATs – at Key Stage 2.) These requirements are discussed in later sections. The most effective approach to summative judgements is to base them on an ever more detailed picture of each child, constructed during the process of teaching throughout the key stage. They would then provide a more informative account of the child's progress than can be obtained from statutory pencil and paper tests.

The relationship between assessment, recording and reporting

Assessment is a process that is closely linked with planning, evaluation, recording and reporting and is a cyclical process. Planning for science in the classroom should be informed by the teacher's identification of children's learning needs and seen in the context of National Curriculum requirements and whole-school planning (schemes of work). The children's needs will be known through previous assessments during earlier work. Assessment takes place in the classroom as plans are implemented. The process highlights the need for teachers to be alert to the unanticipated, valuing unexpected links children make or unusual insights they offer. This is one reason why planning too tightly, in order to assess specific aspects of Programmes of Study (PoS), can become a straitjacket restricting the children's opportunities for learning.

However, this is not to suggest that teachers should not identify clear objectives for their work, clarifying what it is that they hope children will learn from particular activities. When working with children, a teacher sometimes makes intuitive judgements about what to do next, and after years of professional experience such judgements are often sound. For others, the judgements need to be based on a more systematic approach to assessment and recording. Some evidence will be transient, caught for a moment in a teacher's eye or ear and then gone. Other evidence will be tangible and can be retained, perhaps including annotation by the teacher (for example, indicating the context in which it was carried out or reasons why it was regarded as significant). Whatever the evidence, the teacher has to interpret it and make decisions.

One aspect of this decision-making concerns what evidence or summary of it is worth recording for later use. In the past, some conscientious teachers have attempted to keep very comprehensive records. Frequently this has proved impractical. Recording should be manageable and purposeful. Teachers should have clearly in mind for whom it is done: is it for you, for the child, for other teachers, or for the child's parents? Different audiences lead to different records: a note in a teacher record book, a tick in a box, a positive comment on a piece of work. Perhaps a key question is whether your record indicates that a child has simply had an experience (for example, used bulbs and batteries) or that s/he has learnt something from the experience (such as, understanding the need for a complete circuit). Both are important but may require different records. Coverage can often be recorded for a group or class, but learning outcomes need to be included in individual records.

Records will have a variety of purposes, implied by the audiences identified above. Reviewing learning (say, on a one-to-one basis) with an individual can be one such purpose (see Ollerenshaw and Ritchie, 1997, p. 141). Another concerns the need for teachers to evaluate the success of their teaching. However, in the National Curriculum context a key purpose of recording has to do with accountability and reporting to parents on their children's progress. This will be addressed later in the chapter.

Assessing skills, processes, knowledge, understanding and attitudes

It is likely that on most occasions when children are involved in science work they will provide their teacher with opportunities to assess the skills they can use. The assessment of Science 1 (Experimental and Investigative Science) can therefore take place regularly and an increasingly thorough understanding of the child's achievements can be built up, or constructed, by the teacher. The Programmes of Study for Science 1 imply a variety of different activities that will offer opportunities for assessment: observation activities, exploratory activities, teacher-directed investigations, illustrative activities set up by the teacher, use of secondary sources, teacher demonstrations, and, of course, child-initiated and devised investigations. Each of these offer different potential for assessing particular skills (see Ritchie, 1995). For example, exploratory work with a collection of fabrics will involve the use of observation skills, sorting and classifying, predicting and question-raising; and an investigation into why some fabrics are more absorbent than others will offer scope for assessing more sophisticated skills related to generating ideas to test, fair testing, controlling factors, recording evidence, pattern-seeking and inter-preting, recording and communicating ideas.

The assessment of children's knowledge and understanding of specific content will not be possible on a regular basis. A child may only tackle work related to specific concepts once or twice during a key stage. Consequently, assessments related to Science 2 – 4 are of

a different order. The assessment is likely to be limi
periods of time, and perhaps more intense. Asse
teachers to recognise big ideas in science, which m
through a range of different contexts. For example,
of the relationship between properties of materials a..
be developed (and therefore assessed) during a variety of activities
over a key stage. There is ample evidence available concerning the
development of children's scientific knowledge and understanding,
including the alternative frameworks they are likely to hold (for
example, SPACE, 1990–93, discussed in Chapter 2) which can inform
teachers' planning and assessment.

Attitudes present the teacher with a much bigger problem in terms
of assessment (and is the reason that they are not referred to explicitly
in the National Curriculum). Attitudes are usually context-bound. For
example, a child may persevere in one situation and not in another.
Nonetheless, most primary teachers would accept that fostering
positive attitudes is an important aspect of children's learning. Consequently, teachers should at times focus their assessments and
interventions on improving the attitudes that the children have to their
work. Personal qualities, such as curiosity and respect for evidence
and the opinions of others, can be improved through appropriate
teaching.

The teacher's role

Aspects of the teacher's role in the process of assessment have already
been mentioned, such as planning (identifying objectives related to
the learner's needs and selecting activities to provide learning opportunities); the need to recognise significance in the evidence collected
in the classroom; and the need to make decisions about how to deal
with that evidence. This section focuses on the nature of the interactions between the teacher and learner, which are central to assessment.

It may be self-evident that children individually construct a unique
understanding of the world around them, but they rarely do that alone.
The social context of learning, which includes working with other
children and working with the teacher, is vital and a constructivist
teacher plays a crucial part in a child's learning which is fundamentally
learner-centred (Ollerenshaw and Ritchie, 1997). Vygotsky (1962)
offers a useful concept to highlight the role of the teacher which he
labelled 'the zone of proximal development' (zpd). This is the
difference between the level at which a child can deal with a problem
independently and the level which can be achieved with support.
Effective learning occurs in this zone. The teacher, through the

...terventions she/he makes, can be seen as 'scaffolding' a child's learning, offering appropriate challenges, enabling them to build extended or enhanced cognitive structures. This may result from the teacher breaking down a learning experience into a sequence of manageable steps, reducing factors involved, or explicitly offering a way forward. An effective teacher will seek to ask the right question at the right time and to turn children's own questions into productive ones (Harlen, 1985). This brings me back to the notion of the teacher as an active constructor of the child's current understanding. Only by building up such a picture through assessment can the teacher move the child forward.

In the past, there has been a tendency to emphasise the importance of children's active engagement when learning science. Active involvement is important, but equally important are children's talk and thinking. Children learn by clarifying and developing their ideas through talk with their peers and with their teacher. The latter requires the teacher to be a sensitive listener, to value the child's ideas, to work to the child's agenda, not always their own, and to give the child space to work things out for themselves or time to think before answering. One of the best ways to improve your own assessment skills is to audio-tape a discussion between you and a group of children or an individual child. Analyse it carefully for insights into the nature of the interaction and you will usually find it all too easy to see where opportunities were lost, or significant evidence missed. Capturing elusive evidence in order to build up an accurate picture of a child's learning is difficult.

CLASSROOM ASSESSMENT STRATEGIES

Our effectiveness can be helped by having the right strategies at our fingertips. In this brief chapter it is not possible to do more than outline some which others have found practical and useful.

Using a floorbook

A valuable assessment tool for use with young children is a floorbook which involves the adult (usually a teacher) scribing the children's ideas in a large format book. These ideas are usually in response to a key question (or questions), or the teacher may scribe the children's ideas resulting from exploratory or investigative activities. The technique works best with a small group (perhaps sitting around on the floor), but can also be used with a whole class. It has a number of benefits: it shows every child that her/his ideas are important and valued; it slows down discussion and encourages children to listen to each other; it ensures the discussion is focused on the children's talk, not just that of the teacher; it provides the teacher with immediate and accurate assessment evidence (the children's utterances are scribed unedited and as exactly as possible); it provides an ongoing record that can be referred to at later stages in the work; it supports the learner in reviewing changes in their ideas; and it provides an ongoing 'display' to share the children's work with parents and others. Further information can be found in Ollerenshaw and Ritchie (1997, p. 50). Older children can write their own (and their peers') ideas in a science journal.

Concept mapping

Concept mapping is a useful technique with slightly older children. A concept map is a means of exposing to external scrutiny the cognitive structures of individuals (see Novak and Gowin, 1984; White and Gunstone, 1992). It is a means of helping a learner clarify her/his own ideas, and share those ideas with others. The technique is simple: individuals or the group write down key words related to the area under consideration. Each child then attempts to illustrate links between these key words in a diagrammatic form, using lines to show links, with the nature of the link written along the line (or beside it). The 'map' can take any form the learner decides: it could start with big ideas near the top of the paper and these can be followed through vertically, or it can be more like a teacher's topic web with ideas radiating from the centre. With practice children soon get into the habit of producing concept maps. They provide the teacher with a fascinating source of evidence, as well as a focus for discussion (with peers or with the teacher). Comber and Johnson (1995) have explored their use for assessing forces and Cross (1992) has experimented with a 'pictorial' form.

Observation

Alongside these techniques, a teacher will gain a great deal of important evidence from informal observation (a part of everyday teaching). More focused scrutiny through discussion, observation and questioning will reveal even more.

To gather evidence of this type and to have time for quality interactions with individuals or groups has serious implications for classroom organisation and management. The well-organised class, where children are grouped in a rational way which is supportive of the teacher's approach, will be the class where the teacher is able to assess and, therefore, teach the children effectively.

Self-assessment and reviewing

A learner-centred approach to teaching and learning in science recognises the role of the individual in setting personal targets, taking responsibility for aspects of one's own learning, assessing and reviewing progress. Primary aged children are capable of assessing their own work and their capabilities if supported and provided with an appropriate framework and language. A child who rarely receives any feedback from a teacher apart from 'that's good' or 'that could be improved' will not have the experience of another child who is routinely asked to self-assess. Self-assessment requires a child to identify, perhaps in negotiation with the teacher, the objectives of doing a particular activity. Only then is such assessment possible. One way of structuring self- assessment into classroom organisation is to introduce the children to one-to-one reviewing (Ritchie, 1991) with their teacher. This involves a few precious minutes every few weeks when a child sits down with the teacher and reflects on personal learning, identifying strengths and weaknesses and setting goals or targets for the future. Teachers who have put effort into building reviewing into their classroom work have found that the benefits justify the effort involved. Reviewing can provide 'quality time' between teacher and child.

NATIONAL CURRICULUM ASSESSMENT REQUIREMENTS

Although teachers rightly have been critical of many aspects of the National Curriculum and its assessment requirements, it now provides a valuable framework for planning science. To use this framework teachers need to recognise the relationship between the Programmes of Study (PoS) and level descriptions (see Russell, 1995, for helpful guidance on this). Whilst PoS are the key to effective planning, the level descriptions should not be ignored at the planning stage if, as this chapter argues, planning and assessment are considered part of the same process.

There have been some positive changes to the statutory assessment requirements with the introduction of the post-Dearing orders (DFE, 1995). The emphasis is now on assessing children against end of key stage level descriptions, rather than against excessive and detailed statements of attainment. The teacher is now engaged in collecting evidence throughout a key stage to make a 'best fit' judgement against these descriptions which are couched in fairly general terms. However, like the statements of attainment before them, the level descriptions remain untested; they are no more than a working hypothesis of the nature of progression. Statutory Standard Assessment Tasks (SATs) are no longer administered at the end of Key Stage 1. At the age of seven, the decision about the child's level in each attainment target is based solely on teacher judgements.

The end of Key Stage 2 assessment is more controversial and pencil and paper SATs remain a statutory requirement, although they are reported alongside teacher assessments. There has been a lot of controversy about these tests: teachers accused of cheating; levels in science not appearing to match the same levels in English and mathematics; claims that the tests are unreliable and invalid; that children have been confused by the requirements of the tests and the role of their teacher; that tests are driving the curriculum in some schools; that tests imply that science is a body of knowledge (Science 1 is not covered by the SATs).

Teachers' judgements regarding Science 1 remain the only way of assessing the level of the children in Experimental and Investigative Science and we should seek to ensure these decisions are as valid as possible. SATs as a means of assessing Science 2–4 at the end of Key Stage 2 are not going to go away in the immediate future. The advice of this author is to tolerate them as something that is necessary but which should not be allowed to dominate curriculum planning or to change your preferred mode of teaching, whilst striving for more profitable forms of assessment, described above, to improve the quality of children's learning.

Unfortunately, recently there has been a subtle but little discussed change, about which the government did not consult teachers, concerning the weightings of the Attainment Targets (ATs) at Key Stage 2 (now 40 per cent AT 1, 60 per cent AT 2–4 rather than 50 per cent for each area) (SCAA, 1995, p. 27). There are fears that this will lead to less emphasis being placed on Experimental and Investigative Science in some classes (de Boo and Nagy, 1995).

Finally, in the context of National Curriculum requirements, we must not forget that 'teacher assessment is an essential part of the National Curriculum assessment arrangements. The results from teacher assessment are reported alongside the test/task results. Both have equal status and provide complementary information about children's attainment' (SCAA, 1995, p. 7).

Recording and reporting

The links between assessment, recording and reporting have already been discussed. The new assessment requirements and reporting regulations have made teachers' statutory obligations in this area much more realistic. There is no longer a need for complex records covering all aspects of the science curriculum. Teachers still need to keep accurate basic records for each child (and it is probably desirable for records to indicate each child's 'level' in every attainment target) but they are no longer required to keep enormous amounts of evidence. However, there is a professional case for maintaining more comprehensive records if they contribute to the quality of teaching and learning. The nature of those records should result from whole-school decision-making, concerning which records will help teachers do their job effectively, and fulfil requirements for reporting. The most useful records are likely to be those that include teachers' comments rather than those that merely include boxes to tick. Records should ideally include comments regarding achievements, strengths and weaknesses, targets for the future and possibly action necessary for those targets to be met. It is worth thinking carefully about how to avoid making repetitive points about similar children to ensure energy goes into records indicating what you have learnt about a child which is new; for example, over- or under-achievement compared to your expectations. Guidance concerning such records will feature in Book 2. Many schools adopt an holistic approach to record-keeping through profiles (Ritchie, 1991) which are intended to provide a 'rounded picture' of the whole child, rather than a narrow or 'flat' account of levels in each attainment target. These can be developed in partnership with children and their parents and have benefits which go beyond the particular purpose of record-keeping.

Reporting requirements are less demanding under the new regulations. Annual reports remain a statutory requirement, but only those at the end of key stages need to include the levels in each Attainment Target (AT) (teacher assessments at Key Stage 1 and SAT and teacher assessments at Key Stage 2). Reports in other years must indicate a child's strengths and weaknesses within the subject and provide targets for improvement. This is, of course, the minimal approach. Most schools will provide much more information to parents through parent interviews, open evenings, profiles and ongoing partnership activities. One difficulty regarding liaison with parents over science concerns their potential lack of understanding about the nature of science in primary schools. Science 1 may mean a lot to us, but it might need some clarification if parents are to make sense of their children's achievements and targets. Only if we communicate our view of science to parents can we expect them to support their children's learning in the way many already do in areas like English and mathematics (see Chapter 11).

EVALUATION

Reflective practitioners will seek to evaluate all aspects of their professional work in order to enhance the quality of children's learning. It will be evident from this chapter that evaluation of assessment is inextricably linked with the evaluation of teaching. Evaluation involves another way in which the teacher can be seen as constructive. Evaluation involves a teacher in constructing a 'unique' understanding of personal professional activity. It involves clarifying one's educational values and reflecting on the extent to which they are realised in day-to-day actions. Like any learning, this process will begin with clarifying existing ideas and involve restructuring under-standing (in the case of teachers, through the day-to-day experiences of teaching and evaluating those experiences). The evidence to do this will be, in great part, based on assessment of children's learning and the impact of the teacher on that learning. Reflection should also involve a critical look at how the approach to assessment adopted in a classroom supports (or inhibits) the aspirations of a teacher. Assessment should not drive the curriculum, nor should assessment be somehow separated from the curriculum. Assessment should be the means by which a teacher supports a learner, not a barrier between what a teacher wants to do and what that teacher considers has to be done.

At another level, the evaluation process should be seen as a whole-school activity. Continuity of experience for children, the development of self-assessment skills, and competence in areas such as reviewing, will require the staff of a school to be committed to similar approaches and have a shared understanding of the nature and purposes of assessment. The quality of teaching and learning in any school will be enhanced when assessment is a genuinely formative activity, recognised by teachers as a constructive process through which they gain insight into children's current skills and understanding in order to plan the next steps.

BIBLIOGRAPHY

Comber, M. and Johnson, P. (1995) Pushes and Pulls: the Potential of Concept Mapping for Assessment. *Primary Science Review*, vol. 36, pp. 10–12.

Cross, A. (1992) Pictorial Concept Maps – Putting us in the Picture. *Primary Science Review*, vol. 21, pp. 26–8.

de Boo, M. and Nagy, F. (1995) Science AT 1: the Relative Importance. *Primary Science Review*, vol. 37, p. 18.

Department for Education (1995) *Science in the National Curriculum*. London: HMSO.

Harlen, W. (1985) *Primary Science: Taking the Plunge*. London: Heinemann.

Harlen, W. (1992) *The Teaching of Science*. London: David Fulton.

Novak, J. and Gowin, D. (1984) *Learning How to Learn*. Cambridge University Press.

Ollerenshaw, C. and Ritchie, R. (1997) *Primary Science: Making it Work*. (2nd Edition) London: David Fulton.

Ritchie, R. (ed.) (1991) *Profiling in the Primary School*. London: Cassell.

Ritchie, R. (ed.) (1995) *Primary Science in Avon: a Handbook for Teachers by Teachers*. Bath College of Higher Education Press.

Russell, T. et al. (1994) *Evaluation of the Implementation of Science in the National Curriculum at Key Stages 1, 2 and 3 – Volume 2: Progression*. London: SCAA.

Russell, T. (1995) Progression in the post-Dearing Curriculum: Getting a Feel for Levels. *Primary Science Review*, vol. 37, pp. 8–11.

Schools Curriculum and Assessment Authority (1995) *Key Stage 2 Assessment Arrangements*. London: SCAA.

SPACE (1990–93) *Science Processes and Concept Exploration Project Reports*. Liverpool University Press.

Vygotsky, L. S. (1962) *Thought and Language*. Cambridge, Mass: MIT Press.

White, R. and Gunstone, R. (1992) *Probing Understanding*. London: Falmer Press.

10
Information Technology as Essential in Primary Science

Alan Cross

INTRODUCTION

The best practice involves IT to enhance those first-hand experiences which are an essential basis for the development of scientific thinking. It involves children using the computer within their investigations to collect and process information and to communicate results and ideas.

(Hemsley, 1988)

Information Technology (IT) has become as important in science as any tool or material more commonly associated with science. It can assist the scientist in gathering, in storing and in communicating information. Scientific and other equipment can be controlled by computers; information stored by computers can be retrieved and handled quickly, and can be transferred from one place to another in an instant; the form of presentation (ie graphical, text, numerical) can be selected and produced in seconds. Computer applications capable of carrying out functions very quickly are becoming easier and easier for the non-specialist to access. IT, however, cannot do the science for you, neither can IT do the job of teaching science. It is both a tool in the science carried out by adults and children, and a tool for the teacher.

Examples of children using IT in science might be four- and five-year-old children controlling a simple programmable toy like the Roamer or older juniors using sensors in an examination of the behaviour of minibeasts in different environments. In both these examples children are using the IT within their science. What is important is that the use of IT is furthering both competence in the use of IT itself and making a contribution to the learning of science.

IT has been identified in our legislation as both a subject (DFE, 1995) and a cross-curricular dimension (NCC, 1993). Schools are expected within the various Programmes of Study (PoS) to give a variety of opportunities for children to use, explore and discuss the uses of IT. All primary aged children are expected to be taught to communicate, to handle information, to control, to model and at Key Stage 2 to monitor with IT. The UK National Curriculum sets out at both Key Stage 1 and 2 a specific IT requirement across all subjects. Under 'common requirements' at the beginning of each subject's Programme of Study is the following statement:

> Pupils should be given opportunities, where appropriate, to develop and apply their information technology (IT) capability in their study of (the subject).

Within science, there is a further specific reference to IT for both infants (Key Stage 1) and juniors (Key Stage 2). The PoS refers to systematic enquiry and under that heading (1d) reads 'Pupils should be taught to use IT to collect, store, retrieve and present scientific information' (DFE, 1995). Science is an ideal medium for the development of generic IT capability and IT is an important part of science. Thus we have the potential for very real cross-curricular teaching. This cross-curricular approach is further emphasised by the necessity in both IT and science for children to talk, to read, to write and to use mathematics.

There is a slowly growing body of support materials for teachers to draw upon and a list is provided at the end of this chapter. Because IT is such a new, large and rapidly changing area there is a constant need for teachers to develop their expertise and their work with children in the classroom. Experience shows that teachers who make some personal use of IT tend to be more ready to promote its use (Cross and Harrison, 1995). This cannot be overstated. Teachers need opportunity, support and some personal interest to make progress with IT. Activities and suggestions will be given here and in Book 2 as to what teachers might do to develop their personal capability and that of their children through work in science.

IT in science education should be an important aspect of IT in the whole school. There will normally be a co-ordinator responsible for IT but the science subject co-ordinator should see the development of IT in science as their responsibility. Of course, each classroom teacher also has a responsibility to ensure that IT permeates the whole of the child's curriculum. IT in science offers a golden opportunity for teachers and children to see IT working in a real situation where it assists both the science investigations and the development of science understanding.

CHALLENGES

Access and availability of computers

Access to computers remains a problem in many primary schools and needs to be considered by all. This involves looking not only at the number of computers available but also at any physical constraints on their movement such as flights of stairs or classrooms situated on the other side of the playground. It is also important to look at how the computers are used and consider whether there are days when some classes make little use of them or whether there are some classes engaged in topics that would benefit more from their use than others.

Practicalities often have much to do with this situation. The scenario of old computers shared between classes has not yet completely disappeared but the increasing picture of one modern computer per class is improving access somewhat. Children require time on the computer when conducting a scientific investigation and access and availability is an important issue. Another practicality is the siting of computers. Computers are invariably housed on workstations or trolleys at the single plug in the classroom. This is often some distance from where the science is conducted thus creating a separation of IT and science. There will be some reference later on to the contribution which portable computers might make here.

The use of information technology

It is important to remember that information technology includes the use of not only computers but also electronic thermometers, fax machines, tape recorders, telephones, video cameras, etc. IT can be said to include any system of electronic communication, storage or handling of information, be it text, sound, numerical or pictorial. Devereux (1991) shows how teachers can use audio tape recorders to fulfil aspects of the Programme of Study and feels that these 'more familiar' forms of IT cause children fewer difficulties. Computers, however, remain the centre of focus when considering the use of IT in primary science.

Wordprocessing or text-handling remains the most commonly used application of computers in primary classrooms (McFarlane, 1994) although there is evidence to show that data presentation and handling is becoming much more common (Ahmed, 1995). Ahmed discovered when conducting a survey of three primary schools (selected by recommendation, as they were understood to be using computers effectively and widely) that work with data on the computer was dominated by data presentation (ie printing out graphs). When data presentation and data handling occurred, it was rarely associated with science. This seemed to be a problem of perception, with teachers appearing to see data handling as something which occurred only in mathematics.

Software

Many schools have recognised the importance of software quality and availability and recognise that the choice of software made by the school is a most important decision. Some schools have gone for a 'toolkit' approach which provides particular applications or programmes for individual classes. As software has developed we have moved on from the 'just switch it on and put the disc in' level of preparation, to examples like Badger Trail (a simulation program (Sherston Software)) where complex programs can have many useful sections within them. Teachers now need to prepare carefully. With programs such as Badger Trail, teachers and children may want to focus on one section of a large program or groups of children within the class may want to work on separate sections. In many cases the explanatory teachers' notes are of a high quality, facilitating the level of preparation that is required.

Another example of suitable software is Datasweet (Kudlian Software) which is a suite of six separate but highly compatible programmes which will store, handle and present data in a number of different ways. With this software, less experienced children can use the program Dataplot from the suite whilst more experienced children might use Datacalc. Children might be conducting similar investigations, perhaps rolling toys down a slope but asking different sorts of questions and finding answers through using the different programs. In this way we can cater for the broad achievement range in the class, including children with specific learning difficulties.

Teacher attitudes

In some schools there may be concern about the attitudes teachers have to computers and IT and such attitudes may have been compounded by the rapid introduction of the National Curriculum (Campbell, 1993). As has already been said, this may also be related to their personal use (or lack of use) of computers. Many primary teachers have had difficulty with science and technology (Wragg, Bennett and Carre, 1989) and continue to have problems (Ofsted, 1993, 1996). The separate challenges of science and of IT may be increased when teachers seek to develop the areas together.

Teacher training

Not all schools have been able to deal with the training of teachers to the extent to which they are happy. Education rarely appears able to follow the advice that each pound spent on hardware should be at least matched by a pound spent on software and another pound on training of staff.

STRATEGIES

Planning

Making sure that IT is part of science is perhaps the most important step. The IT may be:

- an integral tool in the science investigation;

- a starting point for science;

- a conclusion to science.

Some teachers may, however, be resistant to using IT unless guidance is given at the planning stage. Advice should be provided in the science policy about the learning objectives, about priorities and about the approaches appropriate to IT in science. Teachers will need to take into account the IT experience the children have previously had and recognise that it may be more effective for the teachers themselves to learn about the software that the children have used than insist that the children learn how to use an application simply because it is one with which the teacher is familiar.

IT strands

The strands set out in Table 1 offer a strategy to schools, which they might use to develop part of their overall IT and science policies.

School IT policies often categorise children's IT experience in these terms. It is useful as a school to tackle one or two of these at a time, providing training and spending on equipment and software over a period of 2–5 years in a planned and co-ordinated way to ensure coverage and progression. Science can and ought to contribute to all the strands.

Table 1. IT Strands

Strand	Explanation
Communicating	Using test, pictures, graphs, sound and numbers to communicate, within the classroom, within the school, or further afield (around the country and the world). This can be done by hard copy and electronically.
Handling, storing, sorting and presenting information	This can include the storage and handling of text, etc as above. More often it is associated with numbers. Inputting, storing, sorting, accessing and presenting data can each be done in a variety of ways. The child can do these separately or do several of them. Children need to know what scientific question they are addressing. They can make choices about which applications they will use and how. Children can classify, prepare information, analyse information and check for accuracy.
Controlling	This includes programming of toys and other simple devices and 'control' software for programming the action of working models, eg buggy, a lighting system, an automatic door.
Modelling	These applications usually copy the real world in some kind of simulation (eg managing a nature reserve) or create an artificial or 'virtual' world in which other simulations or explorations can take place. The value of these applications is that they allow exploration of alien or inaccessible environments (eg the solar system) and situations (eg simulating pollution of an environment). The child can make predictions, change variables, ask questions and see the effects of the changes on the system.
Monitoring	In the UK National Curriculum this work is specified for children over the age of seven. We have equipment and software which will sense temperature, light, sound, pH, motion, etc so that experiments can be monitored and logged either inside or outside the classroom. The data can then be collected, stored, sorted and presented as above. For example, children could monitor temperature changes simultaneously in four jars over a period of seconds, minutes, hours or days.

Teachers and children using IT to investigate science together

Examples like the one below are often given. Here the teacher provides support for the science and the IT by getting involved. The problem which will be recognised by all teachers is how involved should the teacher get and when does that involvement become 'taking control'? An advantage of this strategy is that there will be a measure of training for the teacher as well as learning for the children.

A group of nine-year-olds visited and examined the school pond by drawing and describing the surrounding plant life and then the plants and animals in the pond. The children noticed that there were invertebrates, fish and frogs in the pond. One particular frog remained in the centre out of reach with his head just above the surface. The children asked why it was sitting there. They guessed (hypothesised) that the frog liked to be warm in the sun. The teacher challenged this by reminding them that frogs are cold-blooded and that the sun may be too hot so the teacher and children set about an investigation to answer the question, 'How does the temperature at the surface compare with the temperature at the bottom of the pond and on the bank?' and a subsidiary question, 'Does this change when the sun goes behind a cloud?'

The children soon arranged for three temperature sensors to be placed, one at the bottom of the pond, another just below the surface of the pond and the third on the bank. They organised themselves to place the sensors at the same moment and in an area with sunshine so as to make the test fair. They determined that one hour would be long enough for the sensors to operate when taking one reading every thirty seconds. The results showed them that the sensors in the water detected very similar temperatures. The sensor on the bank recorded higher temperatures but ones which fluctuated a little. Thus the children asked a further question. Was this fluctuation the reason for the frog's choice? They came up with a new hypothesis. Perhaps it was food in the form of flying insects which the frog was interested in?

IT contributing to content and process in science

IT can contribute to the process of science investigation and experimentation. IT can contribute to the development of content but this requires good quality software and has been an area of discussion. For example, several years ago a program was developed which simulated the reaction of bar magnets being attracted and repelled from one another (with musical accompaniment!). The reaction of all teachers was that the children would learn far more by first playing with and then investigating with real magnets. 'Simulating a prism on a computer, for example, would be absurd' (Chandler, 1984, p. 21).

Should we be using high-powered computers to conduct activities which are better done using a collection of relatively cheap resources? More than that, no simulation can capture the quality of colour produced by a prism, nor the frustration of a cloudy day if the sun happens to be your light source! Are there not things in science which require the power of the computer and others which can be done better without the computer?

IT in science process (Science Attainment Target 1)

In science children must have the opportunity to identify questions, gather information about a subject from first-hand and secondary sources, measure, observe, interpret findings, draw conclusions and present findings (see Table 2). The first four strands of IT can contribute significantly to these processes. It is worth considering that, with CD ROM and Internet technology, children will soon have huge databases at their fingertips. We already have examples where children can conduct a realistic investigation on the computer (Usbourne Exploring Nature) and where we may be moving towards a notion of 'virtual' science investigations! Again we must constantly ask, do we need to use a computer for this? Is this the best way to conduct this activity?

A number of teachers and researchers (Phipps, 1994) are dismayed that children often conduct excellent science experiments in their schoolwork but rarely examine the results carefully so that they come to a conclusion. Computer databases are an excellent medium for not only the collection of data but also the subsequent search for patterns. This brings us to an area of difficulty for many primary teachers because there often is no pattern in the data!

Robert Johnsey (1991) advocates a 'search for the hump' in graphs which can be applied to any set of results. As you probably know, if we plotted the height of 100 five-year-olds we should get a bell-shaped curve with a small number of tall and a small number of short individuals and the majority falling either side of a mean height for five-year-olds. Such a bell or hump should occur in any sample of reasonable size. In primary science we often deal with quite small samples, eg the height of the six children in a group or the thirty children in the class. Thus the hump may not appear clearly! Johnsey lists data which children can easily gather and which should lead to the production of similar curves. He includes the height of seedlings after five days growth, the number of leaves on a seedling, pulse rates, the number of different kinds of pets, the number of words on a page and types of fingerprint pattern.

The point of this work is that these bell-shaped distributions recur

Table 2. IT in science process

Process elements	IT application
Idenfity questions	Text-handling, simulationg
Gather information from secondary sources	CR ROM, Internet, E-mail, databases, telephone
Gather information at first hand	Text-handling, spreadsheets, audio recording
Measure, observe	Monitoring, sensing, data gathering
Interpret findings	Spreadsheets, databases, tables, charts
Draw conclusions	Text-handling
Present findings	Text-handling, databases, drawing packages, clip art, graphics packages, audio recordings

in nature and in investigations. When they do not occur or when they change from one situation to another there is usually a reason and thus the scientist uses the change in the data as evidence of a difference, eg that bean seeds grown in a warmer environment or with a fertiliser have a different bell-shaped distribution. Johnsey goes on to suggest that children can then look for optimum conditions, for example, for the angle of a slope down which cars will be rolled.

Primary teachers will see the advantages of children using real components rather than computer simulation. However, a computer program might be used to introduce symbols in electrical circuits or it might allow children who cannot physically manipulate materials and/or pencils and paper to gain access to the science curriculum. Modelling and simulation programs like Arcventure-The Egyptians (Sherston), which simulates an archaeological dig in the Valley of the Kings, can provide a powerful context which might otherwise be difficult to simulate or create in the classroom context. Children might then be able to examine death and decay and materials, with a very real question and prediction or hypothesis in mind.

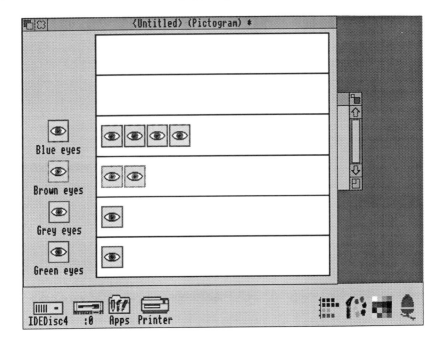

*Fig. 16(a). Examples from seven-year-olds using the database program
'Pictogram'*

Progression in IT in science

As in all areas, children can only progress from where they are and
so the teacher must determine where the children are up to. As Naylor
and Keogh suggest in Chapter 4, it will be useful to involve the children
in recording their personal progress. Further advice about doing this
in IT will be given in Book 2.

There are a number of ways in which we can identify progression
in IT within science.

- Are the children able to exercise choice about appropriate software and applications?

- Are they confident to choose and to have a go?

- Are they able then to evaluate whether the application has assisted the science?

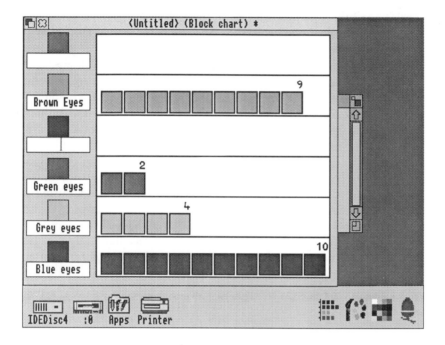

Fig. 16(b) Example from seven-year-old using the database program
'Pictogram'

It may be useful to use the strands and look for progression within
them. Do the steps in Figure 17 represent progression? Beware,
children are unlikely to progress neatly from one step to another.
Progression for all of us occurs by subtly different steps and by
different routes.

All the time children should be seeing IT as part of their science
investigation and so most importantly should be asked to draw
conclusions following work on data. They should be learning to
exercise and evaluate choice in applications used.

Management of IT in science

In the classroom

Assuming you have a computer available for all or part of the year,
you will need to find a base for it in the classroom. Can it be placed

away from a thoroughfare and where there is no reflected light on the screen? Can you provide space for books, etc by the computer? Will the computer be accessible from where science goes on? If you have managed to say 'yes' to two of these questions you are doing well! You need to find ways to make the computer available to children both when they are doing science and when they have completed science. Look for opportunities to include the science data-handling in a maths lesson and text-handling in an English lesson. As one or two children will be on the computer at a time, you need to find ways of maximising the times when children can be on the computer. It may be necessary (on occasion) to limit time on the computer so that, for example, two or three pairs of children have equal access during a morning. Teachers often have a sheet for children to sign next to the computer. Try adding space for the children to write a word of explanation about the time spent and what was done. It may be worthwhile to get a more modern, high-speed and quieter printer permanently available to minimise queues of children waiting for printing.

Consider cheaper and/or smaller, portable palmtop and laptop computers. In a recent project (Cross and Birch, 1995) teachers found that with these machines the computer could travel to the science (in the playground, in the home corner) so that the computer was used more readily within the science. Teachers should not forget the power of tape recorders, calculators and 'toys' to deliver aspects of IT.

In the school

Make sure that your science co-ordinator knows about your interest. If *you* are the science co-ordinator, conduct an audit of IT used in science against the strands. More advice will be given in Book 2. Try to communicate to the headteacher that science has much to offer to IT and much to gain from it.

To develop ideas about progression it is a good idea to select (with colleagues) particular key items of software which will be introduced to different age ranges. You may be able to build up sets of equipment for control, sensing and data-logging. You may require different applications for infants and juniors. If a class is doing science which is particularly rich in IT potential, is it possible to negotiate extra IT access for that class during this time (eg two computers in the room)?

- Simple counting, matching programs.

- Adding items to a pictogram (eg colour of eyes).

- Choosing different forms of presentation (blockgraph, line graph).

- Adding data to other forms of database cardfiles, spreadsheets.

- Interrogating an existing database.

- Choosing the names of fields in a flatfile database.

- Searching for a word in a cardfile in a database.

- Constructing a graph, eg selecting program, labelling axis.

- Searching based on two words in a cardfile.

- Constructing the cardfile.

- Using a simple spreadsheet.

- More complex searches.

Fig. 17. Possible steps in progressive use of databases

EVALUATION

Conducting audits of IT in science has already been mentioned. This needs to be a regular process. It might be based on the strands already referred to and ought perhaps to be part of a wider IT audit. A useful indicator is the extent to which colleagues are using IT themselves both personally and professionally.

Perhaps the most important evaluation is that of the children as they evaluate the IT in their science. 'Pupils should be given the opportunity to examine and discuss their experiences of IT' (ATI, PoS 1c). What did the IT contribute to their science investigation?

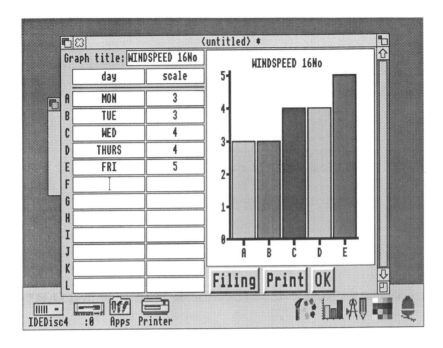

Fig. 18(a). Example from eight-year-olds using the program 'Datasweet'

Play is a child's way of discovering the world around her, and as such shares something of the function of a research scientist. When does playful curiosity become scientific investigation? Perhaps a more playful approach to using computers (not simply giving children computer games to play) could help us to counteract the prevailing bias of the technology, allowing us to celebrate creativity as well as logic. (Chandler, 1984, p. 26).

PROGRAMS MENTIONED

Datasweet, Pictogram: Kudlian Software.
Exploring Nature: Usborne.
Crystal Rainforest, Badger Trails: Sherston.
Optima, Phases: SEMERC (North West).
ArcVenture – The Egyptians: Sherston Software.

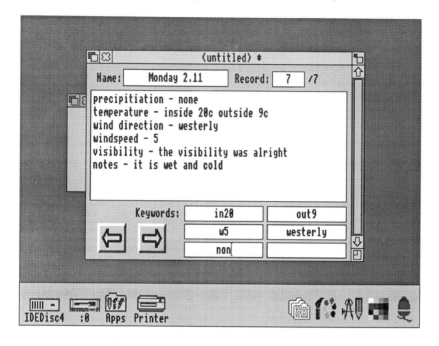

Fig. 18(b) Example from eight-year-olds using the program 'Datasweet'

USEFUL ADDRESSES

Association of Science Education (ASE), College Lane, Hatfield, Hertfordshire.

National Council for Educational Technology (NCET), Milburn Hill Road, Science Park, Coventry CV4 7JJ. Tel: (01203) 416994. Fax: (01203) 411418.

Kudlian Soft, 8 Barrow Road, Kenilworth, Warwickshire CV8 1EH.

Northwest SEMERC, 1 Broadbent Road, Watersheddings, Oldham OL1 4LB. Tel: (0161) 627446. Fax: (0161) 627 2381.

PSION Plc, Alexander House, 85 Frampton Street, London NW8 8NQ. Tel: (0171) 262 5580.

Schools Curriculum and Assessment Authority (SCAA), Newcombe House, 45 Notting Hill Gate, London W11 3JB. Tel: (0171) 229 1234.

Sherston Software, Swan Barton, Sherston, Malmsbury, Wiltshire SN16 0LH. Tel: (01666) 84043. Fax: (01666) 840048

Swallow Systems, 134 Cock Lane, High Wycombe, Buckinghamshire HP13 7EA.
Valiant Technology Ltd, Myrtle House, 69 Salcott Road, London SW11 6DQ. Tel: (0171) 924 2366. Fax: (0171) 924 1892.

BIBLIOGRAPHY

Ahmed, N. (1995) *Using the Computer to Assist in Teaching and Learning Science 5–11*. Unpublished dissertation. University of Manchester.

Campbell, J. (1993) A Dream at Conception: A Nightmare in Reality, in J. Campbell (ed.) (1993) *Breadth and Balance in the Primary Curriculum*. London: Falmer Press.

Chandler, D. (1984) *Young Learners and the Microcomputer*. Milton Keynes: Open University Press.

Cross, A. and Birch, A. (1994) Portable Computers, Portable Learning. Unpublished report, University of Manchester.

Cross, A. and Harrison, M. (1995) *IT's developmental!: an evaluation of Manchester's RISCS Project*. Unpublished report, University of Manchester.

Devereux, J. (1991) Using IT, other than computers, to support primary science. *Primary Science Review*, vol. 20, December.

Department for Education (DfE) (1995) *Key Stage One and Two of the National Curriculum*. London: HMSO.

Frost, R. (1993) *IT in Primary Science Book*. London: IT in Science Publishers.

Hemsley, K. (1988) 'Proving Their Worth', *Times Educational Supplement*, 30 December.

Johnsey, R. (1991) Searching for patterns in information technology, *Primary Science Review: Information Technology Special*, no. 20, Dec., pp. 30–1, ASE.

Lodge, D. (1992) *Computer Data Handling in the Primary School*. London: David Fulton.

McFarlane, A. (1994) 'IT Widens Scope for Acquiring Key Skills', *Times Educational Supplement*, 20 May.

National Curriculum Council (NCC) (1989) *Curriculum Guidance: One – The Whole Curriculum*. York: NCC.

NCC (1993) *Teaching Science at K.S.1 and 2*. York: NCC.

NCET (1994) *IT's Primarily Science: How Computers Can Help in Key Stage 2 Science*. Coventry: NCET.

Ofsted (1993) Technology: *Key Stages 1, 2 and 3 – the Second Year, 1991–2*. London: HMSO.

Ofsted (1996) *Subjects and Standards: Key Stage 1 and 2*. London: HMSO.

Phipps, R. (1994) Data handling in scientific investigations in the primary school: some findings and implications of a research project. *Education 3–13*, vol. 22, no. 2, pp. 26–33.

School Curriculum and Assessment Authority (1995) *Information Technology Key Stages 1 and 2: the New Requirements*. London: SCAA.

Straker, A. (1989) *Children Using Computers*. London: Blackwell.

Wragg, E. C., Bennett, N. and Carre, C. G. (1989) Primary Teachers and the National Curriculum, *Research Papers in Education*, vol. 4, no. 3, pp. 17–45.

11
Cross-Curricular Links in Science

Carole Naylor and Anthony Pickford

CONTEXT

The development of cross-curricular links in the primary school, in the context of topic-based or thematic work, is an approach to teaching and learning which has been called into question in recent years. Concerns have been expressed that subject areas have sometimes been linked together in ways which take little account of the particular nature of discrete disciplines. The advent of the National Curriculum, developed and published in separate subject areas even at the primary level, has encouraged primary schools to reassess their strategies for planning work for pupils. Experienced primary teachers who have found a topic-based approach has worked well for them in the past, have been forced to reconsider and re-evaluate some of the basic notions that underpin their practice.

The criticisms of cross-curricular work voiced by Alexander, Rose and Woodhead (1992) in their paper, *Curriculum Organisation and Classroom Practice in Primary Schools*, are clearly stated and have been widely discussed. They argue that much topic work is 'very undemanding' and superficial, is lacking in differentiation and progression and fails to plan for monitoring and assessment. Although they recognise that 'the topic approach can, in skilled hands, produce work of high quality', their criticisms are at a more fundamental level than simply an attack on badly planned and ill-conceived topics and themes. They call into question the conventional wisdom that subject-based teaching and learning is inappropriate for primary children. Moreover, they argue that primary children have an entitlement to a differentiated curriculum that introduces them to the principles and procedures of distinctive subjects.

Clearly an appreciation of the fundamentals of particular disciplines is essential and an approach to teaching and learning which obscures this understanding has no place in the primary school. But consider for a moment the place of science in the minds of a large percentage of the population. In spite of the fact that people's lives are increasingly affected by scientific and technological developments, an understanding of even elementary science is not considered to be essential. Many people who would be embarrassed to confess to being illiterate or innumerate cheerfully admit to knowing nothing about science. This may be due partly to the dissemination of the idea that science is beyond the understanding of most of the population; a discipline so difficult and separate that only a small number of specialists can probe its complexities.

Linking science to other areas of knowledge and understanding at an early stage in the child's education may help to ensure that science is placed firmly in the context of the child's everyday experience of the world.

In the present situation where the need to plan coherent schemes of work, within the framework of the National Curriculum, continues to be a matter of concern to many primary teachers, it is important to consider afresh how the making of cross-curricular links might benefit teaching and learning, particularly in terms of primary science.

The starting point for any analysis is, of course, vitally important. Critics of integration might start from a respect for the unique contributions of subjects while proponents of thematic approaches might begin with a consideration of a young child's view of the world. But let us put these well-rehearsed arguments to one side for a moment and take a different starting point – the classroom: the place where children and the subjects of the curriculum come together to generate learning. It is at this interface that the need for curriculum linkage becomes most apparent. To many practising teachers it may seem obvious that children's understanding, in a wide range of learning situations, will be incomplete unless links across the curriculum are made.

The point is, perhaps, best made by reference to an example drawn from primary practice. Many schools will have an area of open space or wasteland in the immediate vicinity. Whatever its size or characteristics, it is likely to contain a variety of plant and animal life that children could investigate as part of a study of life and living processes. Irrespective of the starting point or approach, children's activities are likely to draw on skills, processes and content from a range of curriculum areas. For example, if children are to identify habitats, and the species which live in them, it would be valuable to introduce and practise mapping skills drawn from the geography curriculum. The use of mathematical skills in estimating, sorting and setting may well be required, and verbal and written descriptions of the location will draw upon language skills. Accurate sketching of plants for later identification will be dependent on skills in observational drawing.

In addition to links at the level of cross-curricular skills, children's activities will draw on processes and procedures which are common to particular subject areas. When children participate in investigative activities, their learning will be enhanced by an emphasis on this common ground between subjects. Where is this common ground to be found? In the areas of science, geography and history it is within the processes through which learning takes place. Each of these subjects necessitates an investigative approach which involves evaluating, and drawing conclusions, from data. In science the process is known as the 'scientific method'; in geography, the 'enquiry approach'; in history, it is the interpretation of source materials; but central to all three is a concern for the critical evaluation of evidence.

In science, the data may be from experimental work; in history, evidence may be a primary source; in geography, survey data or a map could provide the subject matter to be interpreted. Whatever the evidence, however, similar strategies will be used to evaluate it. The validity of the methods by which the evidence has been gathered will be considered and conclusions drawn that are supported by the evidence. Questions will be raised which may well lead to more investigative work and further interpretation. All three subjects foster a respect for evidence and a concern to draw conclusions which are supported by the results of experimentation, observation and/or documentation.

So, when children carry out activities in a context such as the wasteland example above, it is sensible for the teacher to promote children's investigations in a similar way regardless of whether the initial question or starting point is scientific, geographical or historical. The starting point for a scientific investigation, for example 'What habitats can be found in the wasteland area?', seems very different from an historical question such as 'What has the land been used for in the past?' However, the approach the children will use to find answers to these questions will be similar. Firstly, they will gather evidence – in response to the first question they might map the site and identify organisms living in particular locations; the second question would probably lead them to look at an old large-scale Ordnance Survey map or at census materials. Next, they will interpret their findings – for example, suggesting reasons why particular plants and animals flourish in specific areas – and draw conclusions based on the available evidence. In response to the historical question, the close proximity of houses shown on an old map and the occupations of residents, revealed by the census, might lead children to conclude that the wasteland site was previously an area of slum dwellings.

Throughout the investigation, the teacher will be prompting the learning process and asking key questions which are essentially cross-curricular. In response to this prompting children will be encouraged to gather evidence carefully and accurately, to evaluate their sources and to make interpretations which can be supported. The distinctive aspects of scientific investigation can grow out of this more general exploration of the subject matter. For example, if it becomes apparent that some plants seem to prefer specific areas of the wasteland it would be possible to analyse the soil in areas of the site and set up fair tests to find out if particular plants grow best in certain types of soil. A cross-curricular way of working in no way negates the need for thoroughness and a careful systematic approach to scientific investigation.

The making of cross-curricular links is also important at the level of content. Again examples are valuable to clarify the point. A proper understanding of the place of water in the environment is impossible without drawing on content from a range of curriculum areas. The water cycle, for example, which is a fundamental part of weather study within the geography curriculum, can only be fully understood by children if they know something about evaporation and condensation, content which comes under the heading of science in the National Curriculum. Pollution of watercourses in a locality will only be fully understood by children who have considered the development of local industries over time.

In some contexts, elements of knowledge from different curriculum areas must interact, within the learning process, if children's understandings are to develop. In history, for example, the causes and effects of the so-called Great Plague of London in 1665 will not be fully understood by children unless they know something about hygiene and the spread of disease. Also, without some knowledge of the history of scientific thinking they will be unable to appreciate that the bubonic plague took hold in the crowded and sewage-strewn streets of London because seventeenth-century scholars did not make the link between dirt and disease.

Another example which shows clearly the fundamental and

sometimes complex nature of knowledge interactions is the familiar primary school activity of making simple musical instruments from recycled materials. Although ostensibly a design and technology activity, it will rely for its success on children's understandings drawn from several other subject areas. Musical knowledge will obviously be important in developing designs and the activity will be enriched if children have seen pictures or heard music from other times and cultures, but scientific ideas will also make a significant contribution. For example, the making of a simple stringed instrument, from rubber bands stretched over a shoe-box, must build on children's knowledge of vibration, tone and pitch as well as an awareness of how instruments, such as guitars, are played.

The popularity of television programmes which look at aspects of science using an approach which makes even difficult subject matter accessible, would seem to indicate that if science is placed within a context that makes sense to non-specialists, interest can be stimulated. If we hope to encourage children to sustain a life-long interest in scientific developments, science must be seen to have relevance to other aspects of their everyday experience. It might be worth remembering that until the eighteenth century, scholars considered the whole of human knowledge, including science, to be their field. Science only developed its present exclusivity during the nineteenth and twentieth centuries when it became much more dependent on a sound knowledge of mathematics.

STRATEGIES FOR DEVELOPING CROSS-CURRICULAR LINKS

If we accept that there will be many occasions when links between science and other subject areas *can* usefully be made, the next step is to look at how this can be incorporated into the planning of work for children.

At Key Stage 1 a teacher may choose a starting point for cross-curricular work which does not have science, or any specific subject, as its main element. An example of this approach might be the use of stories as starting points. In this approach, science becomes one of several curriculum areas to be considered when planning. Its position as a core subject within the National Curriculum will obviously give it a significant place within the planning, but in other respects it does not have a special claim to attention.

It is within this context that a teacher's understanding of the cross-curricular implications of procedures, skills and content is most crucial. Providing a teacher is aware of the investigative approach that forms the common ground between subjects – the critical evaluation of evidence – and the elements of subject-based approaches which are distinctive, then planning can proceed at two levels. Firstly, the cross-curricular procedures, skills and content appropriate to the starting point or theme can be recognised and mapped out. Secondly, the distinctive contributions of curriculum areas can be identified and slotted into the overall framework. Although it is not essential for planning to proceed in this order, the approach makes sense for many non-subject-based starting points.

The early years

Taking the starting point of a story appropriate to Reception or Year 1 children, Michael Rosen's *We're Going on a Bear Hunt*, the teacher would start by identifying the aspect of cross-curricular procedures to be emphasised. In this case, it would be the process of beginning to look for evidence to answer questions – a procedure manifested in children's activities through, for example, their chronological sequencing of a collection of teddy bears of different ages. The bears' names, their condition and their appearance would provide the evidence on which to base answers to questions like 'Which bear is the oldest?' and 'In what order should the bears be placed on a timeline?'

Next, relevant cross-curricular skills would be identified. In this example, the skills of sorting and ordering are relevant, not only in activities such as the sequencing described above, but also in the making of a simple map to record a 'Bear Hunt' around the school grounds. Following a walk with stopping points indicated by bear-shaped markers (or even 'hidden' teddy bears), children would be encouraged to record their observations in the right order and to mark a sequenced route on paper. The number of bears spotted would be counted and recorded in a variety of ways. This could also be an introduction to the different habitats present in a school's grounds – long grass at the edge of the playing field; under shady trees; in the cracks of a wall. All these places could be investigated later with the aim of finding, identifying and classifying the plants and creatures that live within them.

The elements of cross-curricular content would then be relatively easy to identify. As the book is concerned with hunting for bears in different places (long grass, forest, squelchy mud, a dark cave), then knowledge and understandings about the features of localities and the relationship between living things and their environments could be developed by linked activities. Content drawn from both science and geography would be addressed through the gathering of information about local features – finding out who lives or works in a local building and finding out what minibeasts might be found on a patch of the school field are activities linked by investigative procedures that will lead to learning in science and geography.

Once these cross-curricular elements have been identified and recorded, then the distinctive procedures, skills and content from specific subject areas can be drawn out. In science, the procedure of fair testing will be introduced through the testing of materials to make a bear's hat for a rainy day. Classifying skills will be developed by sorting creatures, found on a minibeast hunt, into simple categories: many legs, six legs, eight legs, no legs. Children's knowledge of different environments will be enhanced by looking at pictures of grassland, desert and tropical rainforest on a CD ROM. These subject-based procedures, skills and understandings will complement and add to the perspectives offered by the cross-curricular elements. Outline planning for the *We're Going on a Bear Hunt* story-based starting point is shown in Figure 19.

**Starting Point/Theme/Topic: *We're Going on a Bear Hunt*
by Michael Rosen**

Reception/
Y1 Autumn Term

Cross-curricular elements		
Procedures	*Skills*	*Content*
Raising questions	Observing
Recording	Features of the
school locality –
human and physical
Finding answers from
evidence	Sorting
Classifying	Habitats in the
school locality and
the creatures found
within them
Presenting conclusions based
on evidence	Ordering and
sequencing
Measuring	Features of distant
environments

Subject-based elements

Subject	Procedures	Skills	Content
English	Writing process: emergent writing about teddy bears Drama: improvisation – Bear Hunt, picnic	Reading labels and notices. Listening to stories. Responding to stories Expressing opinions Handwriting: letter formation of initial sounds	Stories, incl *Goldilocks* and *The Magic Toy Box* Role-play: travel agents Writing: postcards teddy acrostic lists, suitcase, picnic menu
Mathematics	Using and applying mathematics: data-handling process, practical measure	Counting Reading and Writing numbers Matching Using non-standard measures	Repeating patterns Measuring and ordering objects Weight and height of bears Data-handling: names of bears, favourite toy
Science	Raising questions Fair testing	Observing Recording Predicting	Parts of the body Habitats Hot/cold Wet/dry Properties of materials, eg waterproof
Art	Selecting appropriate materials	Colour mixing Observational drawing	Mixed media collage Mobiles Bear masks 3D sculpture
History	Chronological order Using given evidence Drawing conclusions	Interpreting Co-operating Sequencing	Stories, incl *The First Teddy Bear* Sequencing bears Different versions of stories, eg *Goldilocks*
Geography	Observing, recording and raising questions	Observing Identifying features Directions Map-making Collecting and recording data	Local area – buildings and natural features Distant places: compare and contrast grassland, forest, river Weather recording

Subject	Procedures	Skills	Content
Design Technology	Design cycle: designing and making evaluation	Selecting materials Joining materials: rigid and non-rigid joints	Making masks and puppets Plan Teddy Bears' Picnic
Information Technology	Using IT appropriately Storing and retrieving information	Keyboard skills Collecting and storing data Co-operation Interpreting data	Research using CD ROM – '3D Atlas' Data handling using 'PicturePoint'
Music	Listening and appraising/ Performing and composing	Listening Composing Performing	Poems with sound effects Teddy bear songs 'Carnival of the Animals'
RE	Developing awareness of other faiths Celebration and worship	Listening Responding	Creation stories Festival: Christmas
PE	Music and movement sequences	Gymnastics Games skills: throwing and catching	Theme: travelling

Based on ideas by Ms Julie Howard, Huntington County Primary School, Chester.

Fig. 19. Outline planning for early years cross-curricular work starting with 'We're Going on a Bear Hunt'

The teacher's awareness of the investigative approach that is common to subjects such as history, geography and science will enhance the children's learning in a fundamental way. It will lead to a consistency of approach which starts from children's perspectives, values their contributions and emphasises that conclusions should always be based on evidence. The distinctive aspects of subject areas will not be diluted by this approach, but enhanced and improved by frequent exposure to key questions, such as 'Why do you think that?', 'What is your evidence for saying that?' and 'What can you show me to prove your point?' Whether they are working within the conventions of history, geography, science, or even design and technology, they will become familiar with the idea of always having evidence to support their view.

Key Stage 1

The support for learning in science offered by these cross-curricular elements can be illustrated by reference to another story-based starting point at Key Stage 1: *Anansi the Spider* by Gerald McDermott. In this example, the areas of science content to be covered by a class of Year 1 children would be classification of living things, properties of materials and also changes of state. The first area would be explored by considering the features of arachnids in comparison to other 'minibeasts' found in the school locality, such as insects, centipedes and worms. The story deals in part with the feeding relationships between animals, so the construction of some food chains and webs would be a meaningful extension activity.

The second area would be covered by the testing of different kinds of threads and, using spiders' sticky webs as a starting point, comparing the 'stickiness' of different glues. Changes of state would be explored by reference to the fact that spiders only consume liquids. Questions such as 'How can a solid be changed into a liquid?' and 'Which solids can be dissolved in liquids?' would be explored through simple experiments.

Although the procedures and skills of science would obviously play an important part in developing these investigations and activities, cross-curricular elements would also provide valuable support for the children's learning. The procedure of evidence-gathering and the basing of conclusions on evidence would contribute to the animal classification activity and cross-curricular skills of careful observation and recording would be fundamental to its success. Similarly, the cross-curricular elements of the design cycle – identifying needs and starting points for investigations, evaluation based on evidence – would contribute greatly to the experimentation with glues. After all, the best way of testing a material's stickiness is to use it for construction and making – the quality of the construction will be a primary criterion in assessing the effectiveness of the glue.

Knowledge and understandings of a cross-curricular nature would inform the work on feeding relationships. The idea of distant environments with different characteristics from our own is fundamental to the story of Anansi. The food web apparent in the story (spider, fish, falcon) will only make sense to children if they are made aware of the concept of distant places inhabited by unfamiliar creatures – a

The Story of Anansi the Spider

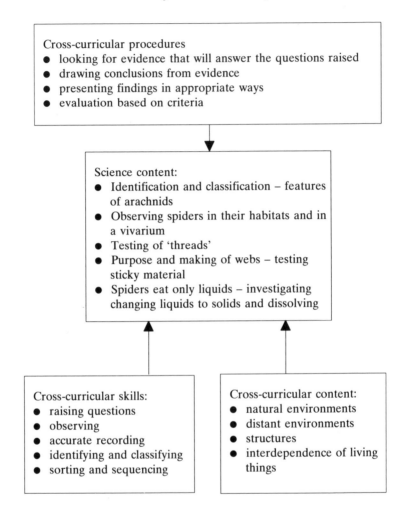

Based on ideas by Mrs Julie Crompton, Huntington County Primary School, Chester.

Fig. 20. How cross-curricular procedures, skills and content contribute to the science content of a Key Stage 1 story-based theme

genuinely cross-curricular idea as it is based on knowledge and understandings which cross over from science to geography. The support for science content offered by cross-curricular procedures, skills and content is shown in Figure 20.

Key Stage 2

At Key Stage 2 a teacher intending to explore 'Forces' with children might find that, although science is the main element in the programme of work, it is possible to take opportunities to make appropriate links between science and other curriculum areas. In planning this programme of work the first step might be to identify the procedures, skills and content in *science* that the teacher wants to focus on. This stage of planning is shown in Figure 21.

Procedures	Skills	Content
Planning a structured investigation	Raising productive questions for investigation	Force is needed to start an object moving, to speed it up or slow it down
Looking for evidence that will answer the questions raised	Making predictions about the outcome of the investigation	Force is needed to change the direction of a moving object
Fair testing	Making appropriate decisions about what to do and how to do it	Whether an object floats or sinks in water depends upon several factors which include the material it is made from and its shape
Taking measurements in a precise and systematic way	Choosing appropriate equipment and using it safely and correctly	
Presenting findings in a variety of ways and in a clear and concise manner	Making careful observations	An object floats when the forces acting upon it are balanced
Drawing conclusions from the evidence	Taking accurate measurements	Both a stationary object and an object moving straight forward at a steady speed are being acted upon by balanced forces
	Looking for trends or patterns in results	

Gravity is the force
which pulls all objects
towards the centre of the
earth

Stable structures are
being acted upon by
balanced forces
There are forces of
attraction and repulsion
between magnets and
forces of attraction
between magnets and
magnetic materials

Fig. 21. Science planning: Forces – Year 6 – Autumn Term

It would then be possible to identify links between the procedures, skills and content in science and other curriculum areas (see Figure 22). Not all of these links may be felt to be appropriate at a particular stage in the academic year and the teacher might decide, for example, to concentrate on similarities in procedures in science and history, the development of particular skills in science, maths and technology and linking science, technology and PE in terms of content.

Procedures	Other curriculum areas in which the procedure is especially important
Planning a structured investigation	Mathematics, History, Geography
Looking for evidence that will answer the questions raised	History, Geography
Fair testing	
Taking measurements in a precise and systematic way	Mathematics, Technology
Presenting findings in a variety of ways and in a clear and concise manner	Mathematics, History, Geography, IT

Drawing conclusions from the evidence	History, Geography

Skills	**Other curriculum areas in which the skill is especially important**
Raising productive questions for investigation	History, Geography
Making predictions about the outcome of the investigation	Mathematics, History
Making appropriate decisions about what to do and how to do it	Mathematics, Technology, Geography, IT
Choosing appropriate equipment and using it safely and correctly	Mathematics, Technology
Making careful observations	Mathematics, Geography
Taking accurate measurements	Mathematics, Geography, Technology
Looking for trends or patterns in results	Mathematics, History, Geography

Content – key concepts	**Possible links**
Force is needed to start an object moving, to speed it up or slow it down	Mathematics, Technology, PE, IT
Force is needed to change the direction of a moving object	Technology, PE
Whether an object floats or sinks in water depends upon several factors which include its shape and the material it is made from	Mathematics, Technology

An object floats when the   Technology, PE
forces acting upon it are
balanced

Both a stationary object and   Technology, PE, IT
an object moving straight
forward at a steady speed
are being acted upon by
balanced forces

Gravity is the force which
pulls all objects towards the
centre of the earth

Stable structures are being   Mathematics, History, Technology
acted upon by balanced forces.

There are forces of attraction Geography
and repulsion between
magnets and forces of
attraction between magnets
and magnetic materials

Fig. 22. Cross-curricular planning: Forces – Year 6 – Autumn Term

The work on forces in science would require the children to plan and carry out investigations to try to answer particular questions. For example, they might investigate which type of shoe produces most friction when the shoes are slid down a slope or test a set of magnets to find out which is the strongest. The teacher would ensure that the children planned the procedure in a structured and systematic way, that observations made and measurements taken were accurate and that logical conclusions were arrived at drawn from the evidence.

Practical work in technology could be developed alongside the work in science and could serve to reinforce the children's understanding of the scientific principles explored in investigations. The children could design and make a series of wheeled vehicles, powered in different ways; from a simple land yacht and an elastic-band-driven buggy to more sophisticated motor-driven vehicles geared down to travel at an appropriate speed. In making the vehicles the children would be asked to choose appropriate materials and appropriate ways of cutting, shaping and joining those materials. They would need to measure with care and make sensible decisions about the order of making so that the structure and mechanism fitted well together. The children could use their vehicles in tests on friction and be expected to observe the behaviour of the vehicles in different conditions and take careful measurements of both time taken and distance covered. Mathematical skills would clearly be developed or reinforced in both the making of the vehicles and during the testing procedures.

Experiments in the classroom on forces could be linked to work in PE lessons where children could use their bodies to experience the effects of stopping suddenly when moving at different speeds and over different surfaces. Exercises which involve balancing on different parts of the body and children pushing against surfaces and pulling objects would help to put the work on forces into a wider context.

The teacher might well feel that a very similar way of proceeding could be used in putting together a history study on, for example, life in the late nineteenth century. The children could be involved in the planning of the project, making decisions about the type of information they would need and the ways in which they might obtain it. When the structure of the investigation had been planned the children would set about gathering information that would answer their needs. They might well make a visit to the County Records Office to examine census information and the local churchyard, consult the local historical society and interview elderly residents of the town or village. They could use a computer to show their findings on spreadsheets and charts, take photographs and present their information in ways that were both appropriate and attractive. The class as a whole would be able to use the evidence they had collected to draw conclusions about the lives led by earlier inhabitants of their own locality in the 1890s and make comparisons with the 1990s.

EVALUATION

Clearly there are differences in the procedures involved in developing work in science and other curriculum areas but, at the primary level at least, the similarities are sufficiently pronounced for practice in one curriculum area to support and reinforce ways or proceeding in the other.

As we have attempted to show, there are excellent reasons for wishing to link particular areas of subject matter in a way that makes sense both to teachers and to pupils. The challenge for teachers who wish to make such links is to be able to justify this way of planning work for children to interested parties both inside and outside the school. The ideas set out in this chapter are intended to provide a framework within which teachers can plan and also a cogent rationale which might be used to justify their planning. We feel strongly that, providing links to and from curriculum areas can be justified at the level of content, skills or procedures, then there is no need for teachers to feel defensive about thematic or cross-curricular approaches.

SUMMARY

Many primary schools still use themes or topics to try to put the content of the National Curriculum into contexts that have some meaning for children. However, concern has been expressed about whether organising subject content in this way does justice to the discrete nature of particular disciplines.

At the primary level it is certainly possible to make appropriate links between science and other areas of the curriculum without endangering pupils' understanding of the basic principles of the discipline. The key word here is 'appropriate'. Cross-curricular links must make sense at the level of skills, procedures or content. Where common areas are not readily apparent, teachers must be under no compulsion to search them out, but should feel able to explore discrete aspects of particular subjects with their pupils when this is more appropriate.

By emphasising the common ground between curriculum areas in the ways described, the essential skill of critical evaluation will be continually practised and reinforced and children will be able to generalise the investigative process to new situations, thus making them more able to make judgements based on evidence in a variety of contexts. Children will be equipped with investigative skills which are genuinely transferable, giving real meaning to the principle that children should be enabled to 'learn how to learn'.

BIBLIOGRAPHY

Alexander, R., Rose, J. and Woodhead, C. (1992) *Curriculum Organisation and Classroom Practice in Primary Schools*. London: DES.

12
Home–School Links in Science

Conrad H. Chapman

INTRODUCTION

Contact

Much has been written over the years about home-school involvements, a term which masks a variety of types of involvement and associated concepts within this sphere (Wolfendale, 1989). However, whilst home-school involvements may encompass a broad spectrum of activities, the main theme is the separate natures of home and school (Jowett and Baginsky, 1988). Just why this is so is hinted at by Rutter (Rutter et al 1979) who suggests that twice as much time is spent awake outside school as in it. It would, therefore, be remiss of professionals to ignore home – school involvement when attempting to encourage parents to play a greater role in their child's education. This educative role, usually associated with the concern of parents to offer support to children within a school or home context, is paramount (Phillips, 1989).

During the last thirty years or so an amalgamation of enabling legislation (Education Acts 1980, 1981, 1986, 1988, 1992, 1993 not to mention the Parents' Charter 1991) has encouraged changes in professional attitude and practice within this area and has reinforced the 'right' of parents to greater access, information and choice concerning their children's school, education and all that that entails.

The benefits of parental support

There have been a number of outstanding success stories here, mainly within the area of children's reading (Tizard, Schofield and Hewison, 1982; Griffiths and Hamilton, 1984; Topping and Wolfendale, 1985) and mathematics (Merttens and Vass, 1990), but more recently within science (Solomon and Lee, 1991).

Likewise, a wide range of national and local projects within these spheres augmented by literally thousands of school-based initiatives, often carefully planned and systematically monitored, has produced evidence, which is regularly reported in professional journals (*Primary Science Review, Language and Learning*), that home-school co-operation works. This evidence also contains some important lessons and points the way towards future development. The essential elements of home-school are:

● a common agenda and shared aims;

● a clear division of tasks and responsibilities;

● a regular two-way contact;

● a periodic review of what has been achieved and what still needs to be tackled.

From these emerge several important issues. Firstly, important elements such as those above can create the conditions for effective parent-school relationships which can benefit all aspects of school life and work. Similarly, a general approach where parents become more directly involved in their children's schooling inevitably leads to specific gains in pupil achievement. It is often impossible to decide whether the significant gains made by pupils in this way are due to specific strategies used within the appropriate subject area, or generally the greater involvement and increased understanding of parents. According to O'Grady (1993), together these form an unbeatable combination.

Finally, a crucial factor in the success of these initiatives is that they are effective in building on parents' role as prime educators of their children. Many different studies and development projects have shown, especially in the early years (Tizard, Mortimore and Burchell, 1981) and special needs areas (Mittler and Mittler, 1982), just how effective parents are in teaching their own children. Parents have unique knowledge and skills relating to their own child's learning. If this is recognised much can be done to use and develop what parents have to offer (CEDC, 1993).

CHALLENGES

Dilemma

Science initiatives between home and school seem to be generating interest slowly. The Co-ordinator of the Mathematics with Parents, Children and Teachers (IMPACT) Project has suggested that this is because parents generally appreciate the value of English (especially reading) and mathematics in their children's education (Mertens, 1993), whereas science education as far as parents are concerned is of less importance. Solomon (1993) refers to this when she notes that it is much harder to sell science to parents, especially mothers, than the other two core subjects (English and mathematics). This would appear to raise the question of whether this can be attributed to the approach used in science or whether there is an inherent misunderstanding by parents of the nature of science for primary aged children.

Thus, if there is to be further development in science with parental involvement, a number of interrelated issues need to be addressed by all concerned (national bodies, eg ASE, as well as local authorities, schools, teachers and parents). These include:

- the development of parents' personal knowledge, understanding and skills;

- the development of an understanding amongst parents of processes and developments within school science;

- the identification and development of strategies whereby parents could be encouraged to help and support science processes in school and home;

- the provision of science resource materials which enable parents to get involved in the activities alongside their children.

STRATEGIES

Starting point

The starting point has got to be with the school and its teachers encouraging and supporting parents to take an interest in science education. Whilst there might be a limit to the extent to which the teachers can persuade and encourage parents to develop their own scientific knowledge and understanding (many parents believing it to be beyond them), the school can help them to realise that many of their common, everyday experiences may already be linked in some ways to scientific principles and understandings.

Through contacts with parents the school and its teachers can begin to introduce parents to contemporary approaches to primary science. Through normal communication networks (newsletters, workshops, school booklets and videos), schools may begin to demonstrate to parents the importance of providing a variety of experiences for their children, and encouraging them through talk and stimulation to become actively involved in scientific activities. These may include the following:

- Everyday activities, such as cleaning, cooking and shopping expeditions.

- The examination of unfamiliar fruit to explore:
  – how it feels;
  – what it looks like when peeled;
  – what it tastes like;
  – whether there are any pips;
  – and if so what colour they are.

- Sharing with their children the effects of cooking raw vegetables and noting what happens to shape, colour and texture as the vegetables cook.

- Raw vegetables may be used in the printing process to make wallpaper for a domestic play situation or to print on a piece of material for curtains or tablecloths.

- Local walks through a park or woods, looking at the different leaves on the trees, identifying them by shape and noting minor variations in colour.

Help and support may well be needed in enabling parents to recognise these opportunities in terms of scientific process, knowledge and development. The school and its teachers are well placed to provide this by helping parents to recognise the different forms of questioning that are possible, eg enquiry and closed questions (Jelly, 1985 and Elsgeest, 1985), and what potentially can be elicited from them in terms of scientific knowledge from everyday things. Schools may provide their parents with frameworks – frameworks of process, knowledge and ideas. Teachers can also emphasise the importance of the science process, reminding parents that these skills and related attitudes are at least as important as the content knowledge and understanding of facts.

All children learn a great deal outside school and whilst they might not all learn the same things or may learn them in a different language from the one used in the school, parents can, with support, help their children to enjoy this variety rather than be intimidated or disadvantaged by it. This again makes it all the more important for teachers to encourage parents to become actively involved in supporting their children's learning and in making partnerships with parents and other adults central to the way in which schools work (Alexander and Clyne, 1995). The activities noted above give important examples of how schools may encourage parental involvement in a casual way within science. After all, a common observation made by schools and teachers is that it is easier to teach a child to read if that child has been used to having books at home and sharing them with adults (Tizard et al 1982). It is perhaps less obvious, but arguably true, that children who have been encouraged to ask questions and to explore ideas at home make a better start in their science work at school. Importantly such involvement can empower parents and improve their personal self-worth. Such spin-offs are also likely to affect children positively.

Involvement within school

Schools must have more of an overt role in communicating, demonstrating and explaining to parents those aspects of the science process and approaches which are within science education today. Parents may well not appreciate why some schools have adopted the science approach they have, eg within a topic focus or the science content being given a more central core. They could discuss with parents the different methodologies, with their related beliefs and values, and explain the reasons for the school's particular preference. These must be discussed and shared with parents if schools wish to get the full benefits from the range of scientific experiences that they are offering to children.

However, engaging parents within a partnership for science development is not as easy as it may seem. There will be those parents who willingly come and join in school activity, others that cannot and still others who will not. Nevertheless, the common denominator is that all are interested in working with their children (Cyster, Clift and Battle, 1979). Therefore, schools must consider developing engagement strategies which range from offering parents an invitation to come and join classroom activities, to developing a series of lectures and workshops or developing home-school packages that help and support scientific activities.

Case study: Year 2 lunches

Recently a Year 2 class in an urban setting developed a half-term topic around the subject of their school dinner and packed lunch.

Preliminary work on the latter led to the introduction of the topic's central theme, involving discussion about what the children liked to eat and the sorts of food which they ate at home. A questionnaire was composed by the children and teacher, to be taken home, which allowed the children to engage in dialogue with their parents – a series of question prompts were used to aid this.

The responses from the above were used in further science exploration, which led to further knowledge and understanding of science. Issues such as what the children ate, how much they ate, why they ate, who else needs the food, where it came from, how it changed when frozen/cooked, emerged as areas for further exploration.

The topic progressed in such a way that a large amount of practical investigation and discovery work took place. Visits to the school kitchen and an interview with the cook were planned. Children were greatly surprised at the sheer size of cooking utensils and this led to lengthy discussions about the size and scale of the operation of school meals and the differences between the content of home kitchens and the school kitchen. Shopping for lunch was a source of great interest with groups accompanying the cook to a supermarket with shopping bags. The whole world of delivery lorries and shopping in bulk was open for discussion and investigation. Menus, planning, ordering, delivery, choice of food and kitchen hygiene figured highly in further discussion and exploration.

Further exploration centred on where their parents shopped and where the food they bought originated. Practical science work stressed close observation and recording of the size, colour and texture of a variety of fruits and vegetables. These were put into sets and then cut up. Discussions on raw and cooked food preceded a study of seeds which were sorted by size. Eventually a seed packet was designed, and then the seeds were germinated and their growth monitored and recorded.

The importance of this work to a child's scientific understanding is clear for all to see, but the reason I have described the topic at length was because of the way the school utilised parental help and support. The teacher had engaged her children's parents through a meeting at the beginning of the term to discuss and explain what the topic was about and the ways parents could help and support the project. The contents of a questionnaire were discussed and parents were encouraged to explore with their children food variety and to take them on shopping expeditions.

For those parents who had time, an open invitation to come into school and work in a team teaching manner with the class and support teacher was extended. This involved the class teacher taking the initiative and leading the work and parents being encouraged to follow what was happening and then supervise their own small group of children. Previously, some of these parents who were interested had undergone a short training course devised by the school to initiate them into children's learning and investigatory work. Stress was placed on developing skills of encouraging and helping the children to ask the right sort of questions, which could well encourage the children to explore their own ideas, and the emphasis on partnership cemented the effectiveness of parent and class teacher work together.

Other ways schools support the process

Earlier it was suggested that home-school links in science, whilst not being given the same prominence as reading and mathematics, were slowly beginning to appear on school agendas. The number of individual initiatives in this sphere continues to grow. The author's own school in Oldham developed with parents, after a questionnaire had been returned from the children's homes, a series of parental workshops on science. Supporting this a series of exploratory worksheets containing practical activities for parents to use with their children were devised. Parents were asked initially in their own homes to explore through the senses a range of activities with their children around the ingredients of a familiar food for the locality, in this case, a chapatti. Support sessions were held monthly at school where parents could share views and initiatives and where the importance of scientific process was being clarified.

Likewise, at a school in Rochdale, each class contributed to a science open day where parents were invited to try out for themselves something scientific via a series of workshops on flight, sounds, electricity, plants and food. They were invited to opt for one or more of the workshops which consisted of children's work, resource materials and discussion of how best to approach the activities within the home.

Parental involvement in the Core Curriculum (PICC) Project

At local authority level, the Parental Involvement in Core Curriculum (PICC) project has focused upon science. In primary school in Hackney a 'Parents and Children Investigators Science Club' was started, running fortnightly on a Wednesday evening. It was initiated by two parents in conjunction with the headteacher, the science co-ordinator and a number of other parents. Financial support was provided by the school, the parents, Hackney Community College and Parent and Child and Teachers (PACT) Project.

To date, there have been eight sessions which have focused on various themes, eg sound, electricity, magnetism and chemistry. The children learn in small, carefully resourced workshop groups which are led by individual parents. Theme packs on 'Living Things', 'Floating and Sinking', 'Electricity and Magnetism', 'Growing Things' and 'Light and Colour' have been developed for home-school use (PICC, 1993).

Later on the club plans to look outside the school for its science curriculum – to Greenwich to visit museums and fly kites, and to the Lea Valley to look at plant and bird life.

Other resources available for home-school science work

As well as school and LEA initiatives, there is a steady stream of published resources available for schools, teachers, parents and children to use within the science sphere.

ASE Primary Science Pack

This is a pack for teachers, parents and children to use. As well as providing a rationale for home-school science work, the pack seeks to encourage and support schools in demonstrating and illustrating what school science is about.

In addition to offering suggestions on how to get parents involved, the pack illustrates the value and types of science available in the home, and out and about. The value of extending school science through after-school clubs is explored as well as the value of getting the whole community involved through community personnel visiting the school and the school going out into the community. An extensive resource list provides valuable insights and information for future development.

Blueprint Science Investigation

This is an expanding series of practical teachers' ideas books and photocopiable resources for use in primary schools. Books are available for every key stage and are carefully structured around the demands of the National Curriculum. There are hundreds of practical ideas, using common objects found at both home and school. Although this is a teacher resource the activities can easily be modified to cater for parental interest. Activities are practical, participants are directed to everyday materials required and given step-by-step instructions. The National Curriculum attainment targets are identified for parental consideration (now rewritten post-Dearing 1994).

Parents' File
This is based on a series of topics which includes ourselves, toys, homes, living things, out and about and journeys.

Many activities are specifically science orientated and seek direct adult support for them. The *Parents' File* (Wragg and Williams, 1993) has several related aims, including helping children to learn more effectively by:

- strengthening the working partnership between parents and teachers;

- capitalising on parents' enthusiasm to become involved in their children's work;

- increasing parents' understanding of topic work;

- making best use of the individual attention that parents, grand-parents and other members of the family can give in their own home;

- improving feedback for parents about their children's progress.

The advantage of this resource appears to be that everyone can see what is involved, yet teachers and parents can use their imagination to apply the ideas flexibly, and all topics are closely related to what is covered in the National Curriculum. The topics and suggested activities have been carefully chosen to be manageable by parents as they do not require elaborate and expensive equipment.

The topics can be done in any order, and there are some twenty suggested activities to choose from in each topic. The format is simple. With each sheet there is a title (for example, 'Portraits') and a number. Various headings provide a framework: the aim of, or reason for the activity; the equipment needed, if any, usually things readily available in the home; a description of the activity, which tells the parent what to do; things for the parent to discuss with the child; and extension ideas which suggest how the activity may be followed up or developed. Each topic has a list of related book resources, which can be given or sent to parents if desired.

School–Home Investigations in Primary Science (SHIPS)

Based at the University of Oxford Department of Education Studies, 'SHIPS' has produced sets of materials with simple activities, which schools can distribute to parents to help their children. These range from floating a bottle boat in a bath, to building a crane with household bits and pieces.

In 1991 three books formed the series, catering for infants, lower juniors and top juniors. A fourth book, *SHIPS: Infant Pack*, was added in 1993. Solomon, the director of the project, emphasises that fun is an essential feature of the activities (Solomon and Lee, 1991).

Simple science activities from the packs, related to the class topic, are sent from school to parents, for the task to be done at home. The children's (and parents') findings are taken back to school so that they can be shared with the rest of the class. All the pages in the booklets can be photocopied within the purchasing school. Also included is a record sheet for parents, which can be shared with the school. The INSET pack available from the authors explains 'What SHIPS can do for you', and some of the benefits and snags of working with parents. Each activity is clearly laid out, with its own notes for teachers and parents. SHIPS tasks have clear scientific content and value.

In one school in Bolton where the author was observing, parents commented that the usage of the pack materials 'gave them greater insight into how their children learn and how they could be encouraged to develop their own scientific ideas'.

BBC Education: Helping Your Child with Science

This production (BBC Education, 1992) contains both a video and booklet to help and support parents in initiating and developing science experiences for their own children within the home locality. The pack provides a brief insight into how parents may support their children's developing interest in science. Parents are constantly reminded that 'knowing the answer' is not the 'be all and end all' of good science practice and that 'finding out' can be as much, if not even more, fun.

The pack investigates a range of topics, including water, living things, forces, air, earth, energy, sound and light. Within each topic a range of facts are given. For instance, within the air topic we note that: 'a thin protective blanket of air surrounds our planet and a vital component of this air is oxygen. Our bodies need oxygen in order to live. Even at a height of just 3.2 kilometres (2 miles) above the earth's surface there is so little air that pilots in military jets need to wear breathing apparatus.'

The factual discourse gives way to a whole series of practical investigations that both parents and children can do together. In the topic above, these range from kite flying to making a hot air tissue paper balloon. The science implications of such activity is stressed and the whole format is delivered in a 'user friendly' style.

The pack includes a list of useful addresses that parents may wish to use in the furtherance of their own science knowledge together with a useful reading list.

EVALUATION

Evaluation of home-school partnerships is not easy. There is no simple correlation between these contacts and achievements. However, this does not mean that it cannot be attempted and perhaps the following advice from House (1980, p. 64) summarises the situation when he suggests:

> The test of an evaluation is not accuracy in predicting an event but whether the audience can see new relations and answer new but relevant questions.

CONCLUSION

The future will see continuing developments in home-school science and technology. The plethora of school initiatives and published resource materials is evidence of this. However, it is quite easy to get carried away with this euphoria, when what is required, through the initial stages of development, is careful monitoring and evaluation of such projects. After all, it is important to know that the energies of all those involved in the initiatives are having some positive effects upon the inculcation of scientific skills and processes with children. Evidence from other spheres such as reading and mathematics is that where teachers, parents and children work together then everyone benefits, especially the children. However, this does not mean we should go forward in a rash manner. This is an important point since as scientists we should realise that because one thing works in one setting it does not mean it will work elsewhere. Schools must be encouraged to take it a step at a time, ensuring that home-school links are in step with the overall school philosophy and are pursued through 'whole-school' means, thereby enabling a general sharing of the issues and ensuring that such initiatives within science are noted through 'School Development Planning' (SDP), which have related 'Action Plans' to meet most contingencies.

For let us not forget, today's primary children will be the citizens of the twenty-first century who will inherit a whole host of problems. Scientific literacy and capability may mean that they are better equipped to handle and solve these. We all, therefore, need to play our part, not least schools, in developing parental involvement in children's learning of all aspects of the curriculum whether it is in school or in the home.

This chapter has sought to recognise the importance of home and school, parents and teachers being involved in the initiation and development of practical science work with their children.

BIBLIOGRAPHY

Alexander, T. and Clyne, P. (1995) *Riches Beyond Price: Making the Most of Family Learning*. Leicester: National Institute of Adult Continuity Education (NIACE).

BBC Education (1992) *Helping Your Child with Science*. London: BBC Books.

Clemson, D. and Clemson, W. (1993) *Blueprints Science Investigations*. Cheltenham: Stanley Thornes.

County Education Development Centre (1993) *Parents as Co-Educators: A hand up for teachers*. Coventry: CED.

Cyster, R., Clift, P. S. and Battle, S. (1979) *Parental Involvement in Primary Schools*. Slough: NFER.

Dearing, R. (1994) *The National Curriculum and its Assessment: Final Report*. London: School Curriculum and Assessment Authority.

Department for Education/Welsh Office (1992) *Choice and Diversity: A New Framework for Schools*. London: HMSO.

Department of Education and Science (1991) *Education: A Charter for Parents*. London: DES.

Department of Education and Science/Welsh Office (1980) *A Framework for the School Curriculum*. London: DES/WO.

Education Act 1993, London: HMSO.

Education Reform Act 1988, London: HMSO.

Education (No. 2) Act 1986, London: HMSO.

Education Act 1981, London: HMSO.

Eltsgeest, J. (1985) The right questions at the right time, in W. Harlen *Taking the Plunge*. London: Heinemann Educational.

Griffiths, A. and Hamilton, D. (1984) *Parent, Teacher, Child: Working Together in Children's Learning*. London: Methuen.

Hancock, R. (1992) *Parental Involvement in Children's Education in Tower Hamlets*. London: Tower Hamlets Education.

Hancock, R. (1994) *Parental Involvement in the Core Curriculum*. London: PICC Project.

Hewison, J. and Tizard, J. (1981) Parental Involvement and Reading Attainment. *British Journal of Educational Psychology*, vol. 50.

House, E. (1980) *Evaluating with Validity*. London: Sage.

Jarman, C. (1992) *Primary Science and the National Curriculum*. Sheffield: The Home and School Council.

Jelly, S. (1985) Helping children raise questions and answering them, in W. Harlen *Taking the Plunge*. London: Heinemann Educational.

Jowett, S. and Baginsky, M. (1988) Parents in Education: A Survey of their Involvement and a Discussion of Some Issues. *Educational Research*, vol. 30, no. 1.

Macbeth, A. (1989) *Involving Parents: Effective Parent-Teacher Relations*. London: Heinemann Educational.

Merttens, R. (1993) in C. O'Grady 'In the Family Way', *Times Educational Supplement*, 7 May.

Merttens, R. and Vass, J. (1990) *Bringing School Home: Children and Parents Learning Together*. London: Hodder and Stoughton.

Mittler, H. and Mittler, P. (1982) *Partnership with parents*. Stratford: National Council for Special Education.

O'Grady, C. (1993) 'In the Family Way', *Times Educational Supplement*, 7 May.

Phillips, R. (1989) The Newham Parents' Centre, in S. Wolfendale *Parental Involvement: Developing Networks Between School, Home and Community*. London: Cassell Educational Ltd.

Rutter, M. et al (1979) *Fifteen Thousand Hours: Secondary Schools and their Effect on Children*. Open Books.

Solomon, J. (1993) in C. O'Grady 'In the Family Way', *Times Educational Supplement*, 7 May.

Solomon, J. and Lee, J. (1991) *School Home Investigations in Primary Science (SHIPS)*. Herts: The Association for Science Education (ASE).

Tizard, B., Mortimore, J. and Burchell, B. (1981) *Involving Parents in Nursery and Infant Schools*. London: Grant McIntyre.

Tizard, J., Schofield, W. N. and Hewison, J. (1982) Collaboration between teachers and parents in assisting children's reading. *British Journal of Educational Psychology*, vol. 51, pp. 1–15.

Topping, K. and Wolfendale, S. (eds) (1985) *Parental Involvement in Children's Reading*. London: Croom Helm.

Watkinson, A. et al (1992) *Primary Science: A Pack for Teachers, Parents and Children*. Herts: Association for Science Education (ASE).

Wolfendale, S. (1989) *Parental Involvement: Developing Networks Between Schools, Home and Community*. London: Cassell Education Ltd.

Wragg, T. and Williams, M. (1993) *Parents' File*. Devon: Southgate Publishers Ltd.

PART 3

Managing Primary Science

13
The Role of the Co-ordinator

Gill Peet

CONTEXT

In 1985, the document *Science 5–16: A Statement of Policy* stated that:

> Since most children in primary schools will continue to be taught by class teachers, the first step is to deploy to the best advantage those teachers who have an appropriate background knowledge of science. They can act as science consultants or experts in the primary school, stimulate science teaching throughout the school and provide help and support for their colleagues. (DES, 1985, para. 22)

Although some primary schools have always had co-ordinators for science, it was only after this report that the co-ordinator for science became an integral part of the staff of every primary school. The role has, however, been fraught with difficulties from the outset. Many teachers have had little or no experience of science in their own schooling and there have been insufficient numbers of teachers with the expertise and necessary experience to take on this role. It has sometimes been a difficult role to fill and even more difficult to carry out effectively. In the early days, co-ordinators needed much support and many still do. In an attempt to address this issue support began to appear after 1985 in the form of LEA advisory teachers supported by ESG funding (Educational Support Grants). ESG teachers were encouraged to work alongside teachers in their own classrooms. The initiative was widespread and successful and gradually as confidence developed science began to feature in the curriculum of many more primary schools. It was not, however, until the introduction of the National Curriculum for Science in 1989 that science became firmly established as part of the curriculum in all primary schools and the role of the primary science co-ordinator became crucial.

Primary schools have continued to be under enormous pressures to manage and develop this challenging area of the curriculum and the extent to which the role of the co-ordinator has developed has paralleled the development of the subject itself. The twice-amended science curriculum has put added pressure on schools to manage this subject but despite these difficulties science in primary education is a success story (ASE, 1994).

CHALLENGES

The challenge to the primary science co-ordinator today is to maintain and build upon the significant progress that has already been achieved in primary science. The value of a good co-ordinator in achieving this was recognised in 1991 when it was stated that, 'The co-ordinators instilled a sense of direction and helped the teachers to implement the National Curriculum science plans for Key Stage 1 . . . Their work and deployment in at least half the schools inspected were important factors in the growth of science expertise among staff' (DES, 1991).

What is the role of the co-ordinator?

The role of a co-ordinator varies considerably from school to school but was defined in 1989 by the National Curriculum Council as:

- detailing schemes of work in the light of the programmes of study:

- working alongside colleagues;

- arranging school-based INSET;

- evaluating curriculum development;

- liaising with other schools;

- keeping 'up to date' in the subject;

- managing resources.

Although the production of a school policy is not stated here, it is normally the role of the co-ordinator to ensure that one is produced.

These are demanding tasks for a teacher with a normal teaching commitment and little or no non-contact time and the management of such an exercise is not a task to be undertaken in a piecemeal way. The immediate problems for science co-ordinators are:

1. Ensuring that there is a whole-school approach to the delivery of the science curriculum through agreed investigational and experimental processes.
2. Accessing time to discuss science with colleagues.

The role is challenging and it is agreed that the most difficult and contentious aspect is the amount of time that a co-ordinator is given to do that role.

> In a substantial minority of schools, the science co-ordinator has some non-teaching time to work alongside colleagues and to disseminate knowledge and skills gained through INSET. Where this occurs, it has a very positive effect on subject dfevelopment in the school. In the majority of schools this time is not available and the influence of the co-ordinator is greatly reduced. (Ofsted, 1995a)

Science has its own individual needs and in order to feel confident in the role the co-ordinator needs knowledge in a range of areas, namely:

- *Scientific knowledge* – an understanding of the conceptual parts of the National Curriculum at least to level 6 and preferably level 7.

- *Procedural knowledge* – an understanding of the processes of science and the nature of science investigations.

- *Implementation* – how to plan (including providing for differentiation and progression), organise, assess and record science.

- *Children's learning* – an understanding of how children learn science is fundamental if success is to be achieved.

The first two are both areas which teachers are required by the National Curriculum to teach but knowledge of the other two are also required if science is to be implemented effectively.

If co-ordinators are going to be effective in helping others it is essential that they have the opportunity to develop their knowledge and expertise in these areas. In Chapter 14 Alan Cross and Alan Chin discuss ways in which a co-ordinator might do this.

When considering the challenge of implementing the tasks listed above, the co-ordinator should keep in mind the rationale for all these tasks, namely the improvement of the standards of achievement of the children. When prioritising tasks co-ordinators should hold this aim as paramount.

Teachers will naturally look to the co-ordinator for help and guidance in achieving improved standards. Science at Key Stage 2 has considerable breadth of knowledge and understanding in its programmes of study and many will find this and managing investigations a considerable challenge (Wragg, Bennett and Carre, 1989). The co-ordinator will have a role to play in encouraging staff to allow children to develop their own ideas and to recognise that this can often be even more important than the level of the teacher's own knowledge and understanding.

STRATEGIES

Short-, medium- and long-term plans

As co-ordinator your main concern is to ensure that the science education provided for the children in your school is the best that can be provided and the list of duties listed above are only indications of how this might be done. In order to ensure success, you will need some sort of action plan, but goals can only be set when there has been an audit of the existing situation in order to identify the particular needs of the staff and the school. A policy of monitoring and evaluation will need to be prepared and then carried out as an ongoing exercise. Again this is discussed fully by Alan Cross and Alan Chin in Chapter 14. Such an exercise should reveal areas that need development and the rest of this chapter is devoted to considering how you might respond to these needs. Books such as the one you are now reading attempt to provide a range of help for the co-ordinator and there are many others available, some of which are listed at the end of this chapter.

Having identified the needs of both staff and school some kind of action plan is required. A sensible approach to this is to have short-, medium- and long-term plans for the subject. Long-term objectives may relate to objectives set out in the policy statement such as equal opportunities. Medium-term aims may be achieved in a year and could include reviewing resources or developing record-keeping. Short-term plans could simply be to tidy the resources and set up a system for their use.

Likely areas of need

Relationships

Good relationships are important if the co-ordinator is going to have any impact at all on the implementation of the curriculum. Support from the headteacher is essential but in order to achieve this the head and the co-ordinator need to have agreed views on:

- what the role of science co-ordinator involves;

- the place and nature of science in the curriculum;

- the structure required to support the co-ordinator (non-contact time, training, resources, etc).

Ideally a co-ordinator should have non-contact time when they can go into the classes of other teachers, not only to support but also to monitor what is going on in the school and assess the staff development needs. They also need time to do the paperwork that accompanies the writing of the school science policy and scheme of work for consultation. Unfortunately in the current educational climate of tight finance, larger classes and worsening staff ratios this is often not possible and time to get involved with colleagues presents a problem. Science is only part of the curriculum offered by a primary school and must take its place in the order of things. Other subject co-ordinators also compete for time and resources. A supportive head can, however, often provide help in other ways. Finance to pay for a course or provision of training materials in the school can help, as can an offer to take the co-ordinator's class for a short but regular period each week.

A good relationship with other teachers is also essential if those teachers are going to feel comfortable in asking for your support and guidance or be receptive to innovations suggested by you. This relationship is often dependent on the teachers' perception of the co-ordinator's ability in the classroom and it is important for you to realise that perhaps the most fundamental aspect of your position is being a role model for other teachers.

Preparation of a school science policy and scheme of work
The science policy should be linked to the school development plan and in order to be effective should provide a strong focus for everyone teaching in the school as well as informing parents and governors. It should be as short as possible, clearly presented and subject to regular review. It is important that the policy starts from where you are in your school and therefore it is essential that although the lead may come from you as co-ordinator, the final document should be written in close collaboration with other colleagues and that all teachers feel a sense of ownership and commitment to it. It has been suggested that

sections on the following are useful inclusions for a workable and useful primary science policy:

- How science is organised within the curriculum (eg within themes or as discrete science topics).

- Suggested teaching styles (for example, published scheme of work, a topic approach, discrete science lessons, constructivist approach, etc.).

- The approach to ATI and investigations.

- The resources available for teachers.

- The resources available for teaching (ie published schemes as well as practical resources; their siting and availability and the procedures for use).

- Suggestions about how science may be recorded by children.

- Advice on planning for progression, continuity, differentiation, record-keeping and assessment.

- Provision for special educational needs.

- Provision for equal opportunities.

- Provision for a multicultural dimension.

- Provision for children with English as a second language.

- Cross-curricular themes and dimensions:
  – personal, social and health education;
  – environmental education;
  – economic and business education;
  – information technology.

- Cross-curricular links.

- Transition from class to class and phase to phase.

- Parental involvement (SHIPS project, Solomon and Lee, 1991).

- Health and safety (ASE, 1990, *Be Safe*).

- How the teaching and learning of science will be evaluated throughout the school.

(Adapted from Cross and Byrne, 1995.)

Emphasis on equal opportunities, IT and other cross-curricular themes will be weakened unless responsibility for these themes is also covered in the school's policy.

(Harrison, 1994)

The scheme of work should be prepared after the policy and should be a product of collaborative agreement and will be influenced by the programmes of study and the classes in the school. Often where there are vertically grouped classes, themes are planned on a two-year cycle. Decisions will have to be made about whether a published scheme is to be used. Consideration will have to be given to progression in Attainment Target 1.

Teachers' knowledge and understanding of science

This is likely to be part of both medium- and long-term plans. As co-ordinator you will need to make a start on areas identified as being of most concern (perhaps areas that are scheduled for teaching that year). Unfortunately, since LEAs have had to operate in a competitive market the INSET programme provided by them has become variable, but expertise is available from other areas. Universities offer INSET both as courses for teachers and as courses individually tailored to school requirements. There are also an increasing number of freelance advisory teachers, many of whom were formerly employed by LEAs, who offer such courses to schools. It may be useful to join with another local primary school in order to spread the cost. Expertise, however, may not always be in the form of a course provider but could include TV programmes and long-distance-learning materials. A series of books has been published by the National Curriculum Council to help teachers develop an understanding of various aspects of the National Curriculum such as 'Forces', and there are other books written specially for this (for example, Jennings, 1994; Peacock, 1991).

Planning

An important role will be to support colleagues in their planning and you will need to be involved in it at all three stages. You should in collaboration with the staff of the school prepare a scheme of work for science throughout the whole school. Such a scheme should address the breadth and the continuity of the subject across both key stages and should ensure that children return to the various strands of science and work within AT1 regularly. You will need to ensure that classes are not trying to cover the same areas at the same time thus putting a strain on limited resources. You will also need to ensure that there is a development of AT1 over the years and recognise that it is not enough simply to 'do' an investigation every now and again but that the skills involved need to be taught and built upon over a period of years. You will also need to be involved with medium-term planning to ensure that account is taken of previous coverage of that topic and that progression takes place over the number of weeks of the topic. Teachers will be responsible themselves for weekly activity plans and should be focusing on differentiation. Other chapters in this book will help you plan for differentiation, progression and assessment and recording (Chapters 4, 5, and 9). Discussions with teachers at this stage might reveal the need for further assistance.

Classroom organisation for science

Teachers are concerned with the day-to-day aspects of teaching and learning science and may need help in developing strategies for organising practical work. You will need to look for opportunities to gain access to other classrooms. This will help you identify INSET needs. Try to find out the nature of any practical work that you see.

- Is it open ended?

- Do children have the opportunities to set up their own investigations or is the approach prescriptive, say through a workcard?

- Can children use the science equipment?

- What sort of science vocabulary is used by the teachers?

- How comfortable are they with AT1?

- Can children talk about their work?

- Are they able to link knowledge to understanding?

These questions can only be answered by talking to colleagues and children.

Resources

Classroom resources

An inevitable part of the role will be to ensure that there is a sufficient and appropriate supply of resources available. Although it is true to say that primary schools do need to provide good quality measuring and observation equipment, much science can nevertheless be carried out with very basic easily obtainable resources. What is perhaps of more importance is that the resources available are in good condition, easily accessible and of sufficient number to enable a group of children to work without having to wait for equipment.

To ensure that the resources you do have are fully utilised you will need to catalogue them all so that everyone is aware of what is available. You will have to decide as a staff where the best place for storage will be. Ideally you should have a supply of basics in every classroom. Basic equipment would include measuring equipment to enable children to measure length, mass, volume, time and temperature and much of this will already be in the maths cupboard. More specialised measuring equipment such as light sensors and pH indicators might be kept in a central store. Children will also need to make accurate observations and it is worth investing in a supply of good quality hand lenses for each classroom. These could be complemented by binocular microscopes, minispectors and magnispectors. If you have prepared a school scheme of work which ensures that topics are not being studied simultaneously by more than one class then topic boxes can be prepared that contain the basics for any area of study, eg electricity, light, sound, etc. If you have a two-year rolling programme of science topics, as many schools do, then such a scheme of work enables you to build up resources over a period of two years.

Published resources
If you are buying teachers' books or a published scheme, be careful in your choice. Consider:

- Does it fit in with your scheme of work?

- Does it allow for your agreed teaching styles? For example, is there a heavy emphasis on workcards or does it allow children to develop their conceptual understanding through setting up their own investigations?

- Does it make provision for development of AT1 skills?

- Do you have the appropriate resources to implement it?

- Is progression built into the scheme?

- Does the scheme allow for differentiation?

- Are assessment activities included?

- Is there material for children with special needs?
- Does the material make provision for equal opportunities?
- Does the scheme include undesirable stereotyped images?
- Are the activities realistically manageable and safe?

Liaison with other schools and parents

Schools

It is important that the transition between key stages is made as smoothly as possible and when the other key stage happens to be in a different school then liaison between schools is vital. Work done at Key Stage 1 will need to be identified and built in. In the days before the National Curriculum it was common for secondary schools to feel that in order to accommodate the wide variety of experiences their pupils had received in primary schools they had to ignore any work done there and 'start from the beginning'. Pressures of the National Curriculum have made this impossible but their difficulties may still remain. If the cluster of feeder schools can all take part in joint curriculum planning this will benefit the pupils considerably as they continue throughout their schooling.

Parents

Parents are often very keen to become involved in what their children are doing at school. The following ideas will both inform parents about the sort of science their children are doing and also give them the opportunity to become involved. As science co-ordinator you may wish to organise an event for parents such as a science evening. Parents could watch children working and could have a go themselves at open-ended investigation. Through activities of this sort they might start to appreciate some of the differences between the way in which they were taught science and the way we approach it in primary schools today. If this is not possible perhaps a science afternoon could be organised where the whole school could be involved in science activities that parents could join in with. You may even wish to write a short guide to parents about the science topics you are doing with an indication of some activities that parents and children might like to try together at home (Solomon and Lee, 1991). You might also recommend visits to places of interests such as the local science museum or interesting television programmes to watch. As parents

194

become more aware, interest may grow and you may be able to persuade some to help you organise a science club, or a fund-raising event to purchase more resources. Conrad Chapman has some interesting suggestions in Chapter 12.

Preparing for Ofsted

Although this is unlikely to be part of any job description it is a real part of most co-ordinators' responsibilities. Ofsted will expect you to have an overview of what science is going on in your school and a realistic idea of where you are and what future development is needed. Remember, they don't expect you to solve all problems yourself, but they are looking for evidence that you are aware of them and that you have ideas about how they can be resolved and who you might consult in order to do this. With regard to science their main concerns are:

- *Pupils' attainment and progress in the skills of experimental and investigative science and their knowledge and understanding of the other three attainment targets.* They will make their judgements on the basis of direct observation of science being taught and discussion with pupils. They will also look at the classroom environment for clues about the range of science being offered and for links with other subjects, everyday applications and the environment.

- *Pupils' attitudes to learning and their personal development.* They will look to see if pupils are curious and inquisitive and will want to know whether they respect evidence and recognise when their experiments are fair. They will want to see pupils showing respect for living organisms, working well together and showing responsibility.

- *Teaching.* Inspectors will want to see teachers' planning in order to evaluate the extent to which experimental and investigative work is planned to support and develop knowledge and understanding. They will want to see teachers helping pupils to modify their scientific ideas in the light of new evidence. They will also be concerned to ensure that due attention is paid to health and safety.

(Adapted from Ofsted, 1996.)

It would be useful for you to use these headings as you review science in your school. Make sure that you look at the Inspection Handbook (Ofsted, 1995b) and decide which areas need tackling in the short term and which are medium- and longer-term plans.

Delivering INSET
You will certainly at some time have to take responsibility yourself for a staff meeting, and it is likely that you will at some stage have to take responsibility for arranging INSET. You may decide to buy the help of an outside agency (see earlier) or you may feel that you can arrange and lead it yourself. Book 2 will have within it suggestions about how you might deliver INSET to colleagues on the aspects discussed in each of the chapters here. This will help you considerably with the content element. More advice about the delivery of INSET will be given in that book.

EVALUATION

If teachers feel confident and comfortable teaching science and standards achieved by the pupils are raised then you will know that you have achieved success. Don't, however, be despondent if things don't change immediately. Change takes time. It is more important that you have a plan of short-, medium- and long-term goals that both you and the headteacher are clear about. Try to get a few things moving quickly so that you can establish your position as co-ordinator and colleagues can see the results of their efforts. Remember you are there to co-ordinate and not to do everything for everybody else!

BIBLIOGRAPHY

Association for Science Education (1990) *Be Safe!* Hatfield: ASE.

Association for Science Education (1994) *Science as Part of the Whole Curriculum.* Hatfield: ASE.

Cross, A. and Byrne, D. (1995) Co-ordinating Science at Key Stage 2, in M. Harrison (ed.) *Developing a Leadership Role in Key Stage 2 Curriculum.* London: Falmer Press.

DES (1985) *Science 5–16: A Statement of Policy.* London: HMSO.

DES (1991) *Science: Key Stages 1 and 3.* A report by HIM Inspectorate on the first year, 1989–90. London: HMSO.

Harrison, M. (ed.) (1994) *Beyond the Core Curriculum – Co-ordinating the Other Foundation Subjects in Primary Schools.* Plymouth: Northcote House.

Jennings, T. (1994) *Primary Science in the National Curriculum.* Oxford University Press.

Jones, K. et al (1989) *Staff Development in Primary Schools*. Oxford: Blackwell Education.

National Curriculum Council (NCC) (1989) *Curriculum Guidance: One – The Whole Curriculum*. York: NCC.

Ofsted (1993) *Handbook of the Inspection of Schools*. London: HMSO.

Ofsted (1995a) *Science, A Review of Inspection Findings 1993/94*. London: HMSO.

Ofsted (1995b) *The Ofsted Handbook – Guidance on the Inspection of Nursery and Primary Schools*. London: HMSO.

Ofsted (1996) *Primary Subject Guidance – Guidance for Inspecting Subjects and Areas of Learning in Primary and Nursery Schools*. London: Ofsted.

Peacock, G. (1991) *Floating and Sinking*. Sheffield City Polytechnic/NES Arnold.

Solomon, J. and Lee, J. (1991) *School–Home Investigations in Primary Science, the SHIPS Project*. Hatfield: ASE.

Wragg, E. C., Bennett, N. and Carre, C. G. (1989) *Primary Teachers and the National Curriculum*. Research Papers in Education, England and Wales.

USEFUL READING

Harlen, W. (1992) *The Teaching of Science*. London: David Fulton.

National Curriculum Council (1992) *Forces*. York: NCC.

National Curriculum Council (1993) *Energy*. York: NCC.

National Curriculum Council (1993) *Electricity and Magnetism*. York: NCC.

Sherrington, R. (ed.) (1993) *The ASE Primary Science Teachers Handbook*. Hemel Hempstead: ASE/Simon and Schuster.

14
The Monitoring and Evaluation of Science in the Primary School

Alan Cross and Alan Chin

INTRODUCTION

In discussing the issues involved in the monitoring and evaluation of science in the primary school, it will become obvious to the reader that many general references will be made which are not wholly exclusive to science. This overlap with other subjects emphasises the need for a whole-school approach to monitoring and evaluation to ensure that all areas are included and that action is taken when required.

CHALLENGES: THE NEED TO MONITOR AND EVALUATE SCIENCE

What do we mean when we use the terms 'monitor' and 'evaluate'? Attention has been focused on them by the need for greater accountability and the UK programme of school inspection (Ofsted, 1993, 1995). For our purpose, the term 'monitoring' should be taken to mean determination of the extent to which agreed plans are being implemented, whilst 'evaluation' is the process by which these plans and their implementation are judged to have achieved what they initially set out to achieve (Russell, 1994).

Why is it important for us to monitor and evaluate? Monitoring and evaluation are not new issues for schools and co-ordinators. What is new is the formalisation of monitoring and evaluation and the specific role that individual teachers and co-ordinators now play. We are in an era of accountability. The United Kingdom spends around 22 billion pounds each year on education and we have to show that we are dealing with that money responsibly. However, education is complex and simple indicators give only a limited picture of a school's achievement. Hence, schools need to produce well-substantiated information based on meticulous records of monitoring and evaluation practices.

The focus of this monitoring and evaluation should be the achievement of the children and all those things which affect it directly. It is easy to become diverted by policy-writing, dealing with resources, etc. to the point that these things become ends in themselves. These things are important and they do affect the children's achievement but it is that achievement which should be at the forefront of our minds. Schools, class teachers and co-ordinators must not be diverted from the basic task of the school: namely, the children's achievements.

Science has now become established in the UK as a core subject in the National Curriculum, and this has required much hard work on the part of primary teachers. When something is relatively new it is unlikely to be right first time. This may be borne out by the fact that we have had to review the National Curriculum within a few years of its inception (SCAA, 1994; DFE, 1995). Therefore review in the form of monitoring and evaluating should assist us to move science within primary education forward.

The inspection process and the changing role of the science co-ordinator

Although there has always been a need to monitor and evaluate in the past, the perception of teachers and co-ordinators has been that this was the responsibility of the headteacher and that it was the headteacher's role to carry it out. However, the burden of monitoring and evaluation in even a small primary school is so great that headteachers must delegate some of the associated work and responsibility. Establishing the role of subject co-ordinator has been a response to this pressure. The role of a science co-ordinator in a primary school is an increasingly complex and demanding one, which has consisted mainly of support for colleagues. This has been achieved by providing practical help for teachers, leading INSET, providing resources, information and ideas, and developing policy and schemes of work.

> The important thing here is to communicate to them (your colleagues) that the only purpose of this process is the improvement of the children's achievement and as such is a mechanism for you to tailor your support for and management of science in the school.
>
> (Cross and Byrne, 1995)

The task is not solely in the hands of the co-ordinator. Monitoring and evaluation is the responsibility of the headteacher and the senior management team of the school. They must deploy systems across the school to ensure that school activity is monitored and evaluated. Furthermore, class teachers have a role in monitoring and evaluating all the subjects in their classroom including science (see Figure 24): their commitment to monitoring and evaluation is critical and this commitment cannot be replaced by, or substituted for, an organisational system.

> Inspectors need to establish whether the governing body has developed a strategic view of the school's development and the extent to which the headteacher (and senior management team where applicable) provides positive leadership which gives a firm steer to the school's work. The same perspective should apply to the way co-ordinators carry out their responsibilities.
>
> (Ofsted, 1995, p. 102)

> . . . a test of effective leadership and management is the commitment to monitoring and evaluating teaching and the curriculum and to taking action to sustain and improve their quality . . . Inspectors should assess how well this commitment is seen through at all levels . . . They should establish what the headteacher and other staff do to find out about the quality of provision and what they do to support and encourage colleagues, to build on good work and remedy weaknesses.'
>
> (Ofsted, 1995, p. 103)

There is a good deal of sense in these statements provided that the resources are available. Schools and their staff will devote much of their professional effort to improving provision with the intention that children's learning will be more effective and such endeavours might be considered foolish if they make no attempt to measure or form effective judgements about the relative effect of such improvements. Co-ordinators and teachers in the future need to take active steps in establishing systems that will enable them effectively to monitor and evaluate what happens within their schools. Inspectors will be seeking evidence to show that these are in place. In establishing these systems, science co-ordinators are likely to be asked to take on the role of monitor and evaluator. It is this broadening of their role which is changing the perception of the co-ordinator.

STRATEGIES: PROMOTING MONITORING AND EVALUATION

Let us now discuss some underlying principles that a school must cultivate to promote monitoring and evaluation.

Long-term development

Firstly, it must be said that it will not be possible to establish the appropriate conditions for the monitoring and evaluation of a subject area overnight; many obstacles have to be overcome. Rushing to implement routines and procedures without consultation or explanation would be disastrous because the process of monitoring and evaluation is merely a means to an end. The end goal, which is the effective development of learning, cannot be achieved without the full co-operation and goodwill of the teaching staff.

Establish a positive attitude

It is essential, before systems for monitoring and evaluating the progress of children in a curriculum area are established, that the school engenders a positive attitude towards the whole issue. In the minds of many teachers the terms 'monitoring' and 'evaluation' have the inevitable overtones of checking for faults and omissions despite the potential for celebration and confirmation of success. It is essential that you recognise this when attempting to establish a system for monitoring and evaluation within a school. If you wish to establish and maintain a whole-school responsibility for monitoring and evaluation it is worthwhile examining how decisions are generally achieved in the school. Do teachers have ownership of policies? Were they consulted and more than that, was their opinion valued? Teaching is a very demanding and taxing job and it is important to have the team pulling together. The process of monitoring can help the co-ordinator and the class teacher to be more effective as areas for development are likely to be revealed. Openness and a willingness to face difficulties together as a whole school team are important basic prerequisites. For staff who are being monitored and those who are monitoring, the initial stages of the process will be the most testing and mutual support is essential. As virtually all staff have some responsibility beyond their classroom, they are all likely to be involved in monitoring and evaluating the work of each other. If approached professionally and as a team this can help the team pull together.

Provide resources and support to do the job

Headteachers must realise that there is a price for delegation. Monitoring and evaluation is essential but demanding personally. Professionally, it is time consuming and has associated issues like access. Who has access to classrooms? Who will have access to the results of monitoring? Co-ordinators need access to planning, children's work and classrooms. Teachers need to be given clarity about their role, they need reassurance through training. It should not be assumed that teachers will automatically welcome this intrusion.

Clarify the aims of science education

Be crystal clear yourself and with colleagues about the aims of science in primary education. You cannot monitor nor can you evaluate an aspect of the curriculum which you have not clearly described. Teachers need to know where they are going before they will be able to judge whether they have achieved their aims.

Clarifying roles and responsibilities within job descriptions

In order to establish roles the responsibility of the co-ordinator will have to be clearly defined in the job description. There will need to be reference to the task of monitoring and evaluating in the job description of both co-ordinators and class teachers as well as the senior managers.

Ensuring that monitoring and evaluation is integrated into the planning and development process

It would be easy to view monitoring and evaluation as being 'one off' activities that may be done at the end of a process or a task. However, to do so would be to minimise the positive aspect of monitoring and evaluating. Schools should establish that monitoring and evaluation are a coherent part of the whole school's planning and development process and should be seen as a valuable means of informing long-, medium- and short-term planning and so ensure that agreed targets are being met successfully and that problems are identified and solved.

> Evaluating teaching and the curriculum should lead to specific intervention.
>
> (Ofsted, 1995, p. 103)

Who?	What?	How?	When?
All staff	Monitor balance, breadth continuity and progression	Review year planner	July for the following year
	Moderation of standards	Look at samples of work across Key Stage	1 staff meeting per half-term
	Monitor standards of achievement	Formal and informal assessments records	See AR&R policy
	Evaluate resource provision Evaluate medium-term plans	Evaluation sheets	At end of each unit of work (half termly maths and English)
Co-ordinator	Monitor subject-specific teaching and learning: – policy and practice – standards of achievement – quality of teaching – progression – resource provision	Observe teaching and learning Review samples of work Monitor assessment results Evaluation sheets from staff	1 day per term for maths and English 1 day per year for all other subjects See AR&R policy As above
	Policy and schemes reflect current educational developments INSET needs	Annual audit	Spring, prior to School Development Plan and Management Plan
Senior Management Team	Overall responsibility for monitoring and evaluation – long, medium, short term plans for – balance, breadth continuity, progression – Nat. Curric. coverage/school priorities – time allocation – standards of achievement – quality of teaching and learning	Monitoring short-term planning Classroom observations Evaluate assessment results with co-ordinators Annual audits and target-setting with co-ordinators	Weekly Once per half term per class See AR&R policy Spring/early summer

Fig. 23. Light Oaks Schools – monitoring and evaluation systems and procedures.

There are many possible models to illustrate this integrated approach. One such model can be outlined as in Figure 24. Undoubtedly, such a framework will help to ensure that co-ordinators are consistent in how they monitor as well as what they monitor, thereby providing for consistency and equality of standards.

1. Gather evidence/review current situation		
2. Identify areas of concern		
3. Generate possible actions		
4. Choose action		
5. Formulate plan		
6. Implement plan	→	Overcome problems
7. Monitor progression	→	Check progress
8. Evaluate outcome	→	Check success
9. Report		

Fig. 24. A model for the implementation of a monitoring and evaluation plan

Providing the necessary resources

In order for the co-ordinator to be able to gain a clear picture of how the science is provided at classroom level it is essential that evidence be gathered from a wide range of sources. One obvious source is from observations of the work of colleagues as they plan and teach the curriculum to the children. In order to be allowed to carry this out, time must be given which releases the co-ordinator from class teaching in order to observe. This, however, places a great burden upon the resources of the school to find the appropriate funding for extra teaching provision which is supernumerary to actual requirements. This challenge is one which is central to the whole issue of monitoring and evaluation for without the opportunity to gather evidence widely from all classrooms the co-ordinator will never be fully aware of what occurs behind closed doors. Also, should problems be discovered in the classroom teaching of science then there is no real opportunity to provide the necessary support in terms of working alongside colleagues who are experiencing difficulties or in allowing them to see good practice in operation. Therefore headteachers and governing bodies need to be generous and flexible in their allocation and use of human resources in this area of concern.

Establishing guidelines for the collection of evidence

It is important that a school establishes guidelines regarding the evidence that can be gathered. This ensures that staff are clear about acceptable procedures so that they have a clear and unambiguous framework to work from. As stated earlier, there may be some anxiety on the part of staff members about colleagues observing their classroom practice, and anything that clarifies and explains what will occur will be beneficial in allaying such fears. It should be stressed that when examining any area of school life it is likely that a range of provision from perhaps very good to poor will be found. The result of monitoring will be an accurate picture of what is happening. This picture will be the starting point for judgements to be made about the direction of future policy and use of resources to support teachers. It will be important to emphasise good practice as well as areas of shortcoming.

How co-ordinators can collaborate with classteachers

Through discussion, staff will be able to develop agreed ways in which the co-ordinator can collaborate with the class teacher. The following suggestions may prove effective.

- The co-ordinator teaches the majority of a class so that the class teacher can focus on science with one group.

- The co-ordinator observes all or part of a science session. The focus of the observation is agreed with the teacher prior to the observation and feedback is provided promptly.

- The co-ordinator gives a demonstration lesson. The teacher observes and gives feedback to the co-ordinator noting aspects which will assist them in the classroom.

- The co-ordinator looks at the teacher's planning and reports back to the teacher or staff (without causing embarrassment).

- The co-ordinator takes a group and evaluates the children's understanding. This should be followed by discussion with the teacher about the children's achievement and perhaps the next step.

- The co-ordinator teaches a group of children different from his/her own class age range to extend his/her understanding of how children learn.

- The co-ordinator teaches a group of children different from his/her own class age range to evaluate the provision and use of resources (practical and reference). A report may be made to the teacher, the whole staff and the headteacher.

- The co-ordinator trials new material, information, techniques, etc. with a group or class of children.

- The co-ordinator looks at a particular area of learning and follows this throughout the age ranges to gauge progression and continuity. The co-ordinator looks at planning and the understanding of the children at each stage.

WHAT SHOULD CO-ORDINATORS MONITOR AND EVALUATE?

Curriculum management

In looking at the management of the science curriculum it is essential that the co-ordinator be familiar with the school's overall policy for science. This policy will outline for all teachers the detail of how science teaching and learning should be approached within the school and co-ordinators should be able to find evidence of this within classrooms throughout the school.

Through the policy the co-ordinator should be able to pinpoint specific areas of concern or achievement, as follows:

- The extent to which the overall aims and objectives for the teaching and learning of science are being achieved.

- That the children are being given the appropriate learning experiences.

- That learning experiences are presented to them using agreed and effective teaching strategies.

- That the appropriate time is given to the teaching of science.

- That the children are following experiences that broaden and develop their understanding, knowledge, skills and attitudes in accordance with an agreed progressive and continuous scheme of work.

- That the environment is stimulating and enhances the children's scientific curiosity.

- That teachers are following agreed planning models and that these are reviewed by the co-ordinator.

- That teachers are catering for the spread of ability within their classes.

- That teachers are aware of and using appropriate questioning techniques to assist children in the development of their scientific understanding.

- That staff have a good and competent grasp of the scientific principles that they are teaching and that records are kept to show when staff receive INSET.

- That teachers are assessing the children in appropriate ways and that this is moderated internally.

- That there is equality of opportunity for all the children.

- That teachers plan for activities to be carried out safely.

- That the appropriate and agreed records are kept and that these are passed to colleagues when needed.

- That resources are accessible and up to date.

- The co-ordinator should examine teacher assessment and SAT results.

- That IT is used to enhance the learning of science.

- That there is a record of any collaborative work with staff or monitoring and evaluation of science which can be used as feedback to aid development.

Teaching

The quality of teaching has been identified as critical to children's achievement. It may be surprising to find that a number of teachers have little experience in articulating their teaching. Newly qualified teachers should have used teaching competencies on any recent course of training and may have a career entry profile. For them this will be a good starting point. Such a framework may prove useful to more experienced teachers. For example:

Five dimensions of teaching competence
1. Understanding of the whole curriculum
2. Subject knowledge and application
3. Assessment and recording of pupils' progress
4. Teaching strategies
5. Further professional development.

(DFE, 1993)

Under dimension 4, newly qualified teachers should be able to:

- establish clear expectations of pupil behaviour in the classroom and secure appropriate standards of discipline;

- create and maintain a purposeful, orderly and supportive environment for their pupils' learning;

- maintain pupils' interest and motivation;

- present learning tasks and curriculum content in a clear and stimulating manner;

- teach whole classes, groups and individuals, and determine the most appropriate learning goals and classroom contexts for using these and other strategies;

- use a range of teaching techniques, and judge how to deploy them;

- employ varying forms of curriculum organisation, and monitor their effectiveness;

- communicate clearly and effectively with pupils through questioning, instructing and feedback;

- select and use a range of resources for learning, including information technology;

- train pupils in the individual and collaborative study skills necessary for effective learning.

This should not be used as a checklist but rather as an aide memoire and an agenda for development.

Pupil achievement

The central driving force for all the efforts of the staff in the school must be the attainment of the children. All aspects of the school should be working towards this one goal. Co-ordinators must therefore be aware of the children's achievements at all levels. Class teachers are required to assess and maintain records of their children's achievement. This information can be gathered in a variety of ways and should be compared both within the school and to national standards. For example, the co-ordinator may wish to view a range of work from any given year and view this according to levels of achievement. Work can be judged against school-based portfolios to gauge levels of attainment thus giving some idea of how well pupils are performing in relation to national levels and whether this performance is high, average or low. It will also allow the co-ordinator to ensure that appropriate standards of presentation and layout in the children's work are maintained. Dated work will give some idea of pace and regularity. Evidence can also be gathered from the children's work of difficulties experienced, and some idea gained of how these difficulties were overcome. Provision for the most able can also be checked in this fashion. Other information can be gained from the class teacher's own records for the class as a whole and from Standard Assessment Test and teacher assessment results. Such information would identify any pupils with special needs, either low or high achievers.

Evidence from formal assessments given by the class teacher can be used to check the achievement of pupils. These may be focused on specific areas of understanding or on specific aspects of the investigative process. The co-ordinator may wish to question children informally to find out what they have learnt or set them a task and observe them as they carry it out so as to gauge their competency in the planning, execution and follow up of an experiment.

Financial management

In the area of financial management the co-ordinator will need to monitor and assess the use of funds allocated to the science budget. Co-ordinators should have a clear idea of short-term and long-term needs and priorities. These should be stated prior to the initial stages of the setting of the school budget for the ensuing year, take into account previous priorities, and dovetail with the school's development plan. Co-ordinators will need to determine from colleagues their immediate needs together with long-term requests. These can then be prioritised according to the focus for the coming year. Should additional funds become available co-ordinators may then be able to satisfy the long-term needs in advance of the planned programme of spending.

As co-ordinators make use of the funds, they should have access to the status of their budget on a regular basis so as to be aware of their outgoings.

Professional development

An area that is usually neglected in any review of the curriculum is the development of the co-ordinator's own professional expertise. Co-ordinators may have the opportunity to be involved in the planning of their own professional development and this could be staged to coincide with the school's development plan. If the school has a clear idea of when curriculum initiatives are to be implemented this will allow the co-ordinator an opportunity to gain expertise and support prior to the start of the programme. Such opportunities could be of a long-term nature, such as a diploma of attendance or other professionally recognised forms of study, or they may be of a shorter duration such as LEA courses or co-ordinator update meetings. Such forms of professional development can be logged by the co-ordinator so as to provide an ongoing record of the update of skills and knowledge. Should other staff attend INSET related to science these too may be logged to provide evidence of the commitment of the school to developing the skills and knowledge of the staff in the teaching and learning of primary science.

EVALUATION

To talk of monitoring and evaluation of a monitoring and evaluation policy might be to invite ridicule. However, the school and its staff need information to determine how well the school is doing. The monitoring and evaluation policy must itself come under scrutiny. This is the responsibility of the head and the senior management team but should involve the staff.

- Are you able to judge your success?

- Are problems easy to identify?

- Are you then able to do something about them?

- Are there examples of the policy resulting in change for the better?

- Is this an effective use of your time?

- Do teachers see it as a positive vehicle for developing them professionally?

If the answer is not a firm 'yes' to any of these then it may be time for such a review. It would be important to conduct such a review in the first year of a new policy and then at least every second year following that.

CONCLUSION

The monitoring and evaluation of any curriculum area is an issue that needs careful and thoughtful planning. It should be part of a whole-school approach and should be developed through the staff of the school concerned. Everyone must come to recognise their role in the process and the part that it plays in guiding the school in its future development. As schools move towards the new millennium it is clear that there are many challenges yet to be faced. Co-ordinators of all curriculum areas have found that their roles are changing. In times of change the only certainty is that there will be further changes to follow. Co- ordinators are rising to these challenges when they are supported by headteachers and by being flexible and open-minded. Where they are required to take on the task of monitoring and evaluating the development and progress of their subject they will need to show considerable resourcefulness.

BIBLIOGRAPHY

Cross, A. and Byrne, D. (1995) Co-ordinating Science at Key Stage 2, in M. Harrison (ed.) *Developing a Leadership Role in Key Stage 2 Curriculum.* London: Falmer Press.

DFE (1993) *Circular 14/93.* London: HMSO.

DFE (1995) *Science in the National Curriculum.* London: HMSO.

Hargreaves, D. et al (1989) *Schools Development Plans Project – Planning for School Development Advice to Governors, Headteachers and Teachers.* London: HMSO.

Hooper, R. (ed.) (1973) *The Curriculum: Context, Design and Development.* Edinburgh: Oliver & Boyd.

Kelly, A. V. (1989) *The Curriculum Theory and Practice.* London: Paul Chapman.

National Curriculum Council (1993) *Planning the National Curriculum at Key Stage 2.* York: NCC.

Ofsted (1993) *The Handbook for the Inspection of Schools.* London: HMSO.

Ofsted (1995) *a. Framework for the Inspection of Schools.* London: HMSO. *b. Guidance on the Inspection of Nursery and Primary Schools.* London: HMSO.

Russell, S. (1994) *Ready for Action: a Practical Guide to Post-Ofsted Action Planning.* Leamington Spa: Courseware Publications.

Schools Curriculum and Assessment Authority (1995) *Planning the Curriculum at Key Stages 1 and 2.* London: SCAA.

Schools Curriculum and Assessment Authority (1994) *Science in the National Curriculum: Draft Proposals.* London: SCAA.

Index

Art, 96, 117, 143
audit, 188
annotations, 30
anti-racism, 77, 78
assessment, 21, 30, 85, 90, 103,
    122–33
  assessment and record
    keeping, 53
  formative, 123, 133
  teaching, learning and
    assessment, 54
  self-assessment, 130, 133
  statutory assessment, 20, 122,
    123, 125, 130, 131, 209
  summative, 123, 124
Attainment targets, 108, 115,
    131, 132, 177, 195
  Attainment Target 1, 56, 59,
    106–21, 142, 191
attitudes, 17, 23, 126–7, 169,
    172, 201

classrooms, 33, 106, 107, 115
  management, 94
  organisation, 129, 130, 192
  resources, 192–3
concepts, 16, 17, 18, 20, 21, 59,
    94, 95, 97, 103, 105
  concept keyboard, 70
  concept maps, 54, 129
  conceptual development, 51,
    59

scientific concepts, 18, 20
constructivism, 26, 108
  constructivist approach to
    teaching and learning, 24,
    25, 26, 27, 29, 34, 86, 124,
    127
communication, 72, 73, 102,
    110
computers, 137, 138, 139, 142,
    147, 149, 150
co-ordinator, 19, 23, 136, 176,
    169–80, 199, 200, 201, 204,
    205, 206, 207, 209, 210
curriculum, 59, 62, 81–2, 83–5,
    123, 131, 132, 133, 137, 138,
    143, 152, 153, 154, 155, 156,
    157, 163, 167, 168, 176, 180,
    187, 189, 190, 194, 199, 200,
    201, 202, 206, 207, 208, 209,
    210, 211
cross-curricular, 21, 136, 152,
    168

Dearing, 53, 62, 107, 110, 123,
    130, 177
differentiation, 21, 52, 64–74,
    123–4, 152, 192
  task, 65, 67, 68
  outcome, 65, 67, 68
discussion, 21, 55, 100, 128, 129,
    174–5, 195
drawings, 29, 54, 55, 96

early years, 16, 22, 80, 93, 95, 104, 157, 170
English, 76, 77, 81, 85, 86, 88, 113, 117, 131, 133, 146, 171
electricity, 40, 46, 89
environment, 83, 91, 101, 107, 108, 140, 143
equal opportunities, 21, 76, 78, 81, 83, 86, 90, 188, 190, 191, 194
equipment, 135, 139, 140, 148, 177, 192, 193
evaluation, 15, 20, 22, 114, 124, 125, 198–211
experiment, 96, 100, 110, 111, 112, 114

fair testing, 57, 103, 109, 115, 120, 126, 158
floorbook, 128
food, 83, 85, 88, 89, 141, 161, 174–5
forces, 40, 43–4, 166–7, 178

gender, 78, 84, 87, 91
group work, 101

history, 154, 155, 160, 164, 166
  scientists of history, 16
home-school, 22, 169–80
hypothesis, 57, 106, 112, 130, 141, 144
HMI, 19, 65, 100

ideas, 16, 24, 37
  alternative ideas, 18, 34
  children's ideas, 20–34, 39, 51, 52, 53, 55, 58, 59, 65, 68, 93, 94, 97, 99, 100, 101, 102, 108, 109, 112, 124, 126, 128, 129, 133
  developing children's ideas, 53, 54, 55, 56, 62
  elicitation of ideas, 29, 52, 99
  expression of ideas, 29
  personal ideas, 18
  scientific ideas, 20, 37, 38, 47, 53, 58, 59, 62, 96, 106, 107, 108, 127
information technology, 22, 135, 136, 137, 190, 208
  control, 136, 149
  data-base, 145, 147
  modelling, 140, 144
  software, 146, 148
  word processing, 137
  (*see* computers)
INSET, 94, 107, 110, 191, 192, 196, 210
inspection, 198, 199
inspector, 189, 195
investigations, 30, 31, 35, 55, 56, 58, 59, 68, 69, 83, 87, 88, 94, 96, 97, 101, 112, 113, 114, 117, 120, 126, 137, 139, 141, 142, 146, 150, 154, 155, 167, 174, 176, 187, 188, 190, 192, 193, 194

Key stages, 58, 115, 126, 127, 130, 131, 176, 194
  Key Stage 1, 87, 88, 96, 97, 102, 106, 112, 114, 131, 132, 156, 161, 186, 194
  Key Stage 2, 89, 106, 112, 131, 132, 163, 188
knowledge and understanding, 18, 23, 24, 26, 27, 28, 34, 53, 59, 153, 155, 156, 157, 158, 161, 185, 187, 191
  scientific knowledge, 17, 21, 30, 35, 96, 106, 107
  subject knowledge, 19, 21, 22, 93, 94, 95, 108, 115

language, 17, 20, 70, 76, 100, 154
  acquisition and development,
    22
language and learning, 37–48
second language speakers, 77,
  81, 82, 84, 86, 190
learning, 22, 64, 65, 68, 70, 71,
  72, 73, 191, 195
  learning activities,, 27, 30, 65
  learning difficulties, 67, 138
  learning outcomes, 26, 115,
    117
  learning process, 24, 25, 30,
    39, 44, 155
  learning theorists, 26, 107
  children's learning, 24, 30, 34,
    35, 40, 54, 62, 65, 67, 100,
    101, 104, 108, 122–8, 130,
    131, 132, 133, 154
  progression in learning, 51–63
  scientific learning, 22, 34, 38,
    43, 62, 65
✳ teaching and learning, 15, 20,
    24, 26, 30, 34, 38, 43, 54, 67,
    71, 152, 153, 192

mathematics, 70, 113, 131, 133,
  136, 138, 156, 166, 170, 171,
  175, 179
monitoring, 19, 69, 72, 140, 143,
  152, 179, 188
multicultural, 77, 86, 88, 90, 91,
  190

National Curriculum
  Programmes of Study, 58,
  103, 107, 115, 117, 125, 126,
  130, 136, 191

observation, 69, 96, 97, 107,
  111, 116, 126, 129, 154, 161,
  174

OFSTED, 64, 65, 101, 195

planning, 19, 52, 53, 56, 58, 59,
  62, 86, 94, 102, 103–4, 113,
  115, 125, 127, 130, 131, 139,
  152, 156, 157, 158, 163, 167,
  195, 202
  children's planning, 117, 120,
    167
  short, medium, long term, 55,
    188, 191, 192, 196
practical work, 57, 82, 95, 96,
  97, 103, 104, 110, 111, 116,
  117, 120, 166, 192, 205
prediction, 109, 112, 113, 114,
  120
problem solving, 96, 97, 99
process
  assessment process, 124, 125,
    127, 130
  process based learning, 82, 86,
    90
  process skills, 21, 59, 86, 107
  language process, 40, 41, 43,
    44, 47
  learning process, 24, 25, 26,
    30, 38, 44, 52
  teaching process, 21
  scientific process, 21, 30, 59,
    112
progression, 21, 51–63, 94, 115,
  123, 131, 140, 146, 148, 152,
  187, 190, 191, 192, 193

questions and questioning, 17,
  27–9, 69, 94, 95, 99, 117, 128
  children's questions, 15, 33,
    57, 99, 138, 140, 142
  scientific questions, 17, 30

records, 56, 125, 126, 132, 199,
  207, 208, 209

resources, 116, 142, 176, 186, 188, 189, 190, 192–3, 199, 202, 204, 206, 207, 208
reporting, 122, 123, 125, 126, 132
results, 82, 111, 113, 114, 120, 124, 125, 131, 135, 141, 142, 154

safety, 190, 195
school development plan, 189
sound, 29, 31, 137, 140, 176, 178
space, 40–1
scheme of work, 53, 189, 190, 191, 193
special educational needs, 103, 190
stories, 156
⚹ subjects, 21, 136, 157, 160, 168, 171

⚹teaching, 38, 40, 46, 48, 54, 58, 67, 71, 91, 93, 94, 95, 101, 130, 131, 152, 153
teacher's role, 127–8
strategies, 87, 95, 195, 206, 207
technology, 80, 85, 117, 156, 160, 164, 166, 179
topics, 137, 152, 168, 177, 178, 193, 194
themes, 152, 168, 176, 190, 191

variables, 106, 112, 113
vocabulary, 17, 18, 37–9, 43, 46, 47, 100

whole-school, 132, 136, 187, 191, 194, 198, 201, 211

More *Resources in Education* Titles from Northcote House

The following pages contain details of a selection of other titles from the *Resources in Education* series. For further information, and details of our Inspection Copy Service, please apply to:

Northcote House Publishers Ltd, Plymbridge House, Estover Road, Plymouth PL6 7PY, United Kingdom. Tel: Plymouth (01752) 202301. Fax: (01752) 202330.

A selection of catalogues and brochures is usually available on request.

Beyond the Core Curriculum
Co-Ordinating the Other Foundation Subjects in Primary Schools

EDITED BY
MIKE HARRISON

To help schools to meet the needs of the National Curriculum, primary teachers are required increasingly to act as consultants to their colleagues in particular subjects. This task of curriculum co-ordination often demands a new range of skills from teachers whose expertise may, hitherto, have been confined mainly to classroom teaching.

This practical book helps those charged with leading their school's staff in: Geography, History, Physical Education, Information Technology, Music, Art and Design, Technology, and Religious Education to develop their subject knowledge, network with others and find ways to influence colleagues to ensure that their subject is taught imaginatively and coherently in the school.

Written by a team of primary specialists this book offers invaluable advice and support to headteachers, teachers and students for whom the co-ordination of the foundation subjects in primary schools is an area of growing interest and responsibility.

The Editor, Mike Harrison, is Director of the Centre for Primary Education in the University of Manchester. He has worked as a primary teacher and a headteacher, leads primary pre-service education and is currently running inter-LEA courses for primary co-ordinators. He is known nationally for his courses on education management for prospective primary deputy heads. He is co-author of *Primary School Management* (Heinemann, 1992).

The ten co-authors are all primary experts in their fields, many running twenty-day training courses for primary co-ordinators in their subjects.

Paperback, 192 pages, tables.

The Language of Discipline
A practical approach to effective classroom management
Second Edition

BILL ROGERS

All teachers at some point in their careers encounter discipline problems in the classroom. Newly qualified and trainee teachers, in particular, often find classroom control the most demanding aspect of their new profession.

In this highly practical and user-friendly handbook Bill Rogers shows, step-by-step, how to draw up an effective discipline plan and strike the right balance between encouragement and correction. Good discipline does not just happen but is the product of careful planning, behaviour analysis, and the appropriate use of language and assertive skills. This book addresses all forms of disruptive behaviour, especially hostile and argumentative students, and shows that it is possible for every teacher, however inexperienced, to establish effective control and provide the right learning environment for the entire class. It will be welcomed by all teachers seeking a long-term positive solution to the demanding problem of disruptive behaviour in the classroom.

Bill Rogers is an education consultant specialising in classroom discipline and management, and teacher peer support. He was consultant to the *Elton Report: Discipline in Schools* (1989) and to the Victoria Ministry of Education (1985–88). He has taught at every level of education and written many articles and several books on discipline, teacher stress and teacher welfare including: *You Know the Fair Rule* (Longman, 1991), *Supporting Teachers in the Workplace* (Jacaranda, 1992), and *Making a Discipline Plan* (Nelson, 1989). He now lectures and runs INSET course in Australia and the United Kingdom where he is attached annually to the University of Cambridge Institute of Education to run in-service programmes on discipline and peer support for teachers.

Paperback, 176 pages, tables.

Managing Stress in Schools
A practical guide to effective strategies for teachers

MARIE BROWN & SUE RALPH

Managing stress is a growing problem for teachers in schools as they seek to meet the increasing demands of the National Curriculum, local management of schools (LMS), and the rising expectations of parents understandably wanting quantifiable examination results for their children approaching the highly competitive labour or higher education markets for the first time.

Based on sound psychological theory and research the emphasis of this book is, throughout, on practical solutions to teacher stress. Its sound analysis and realistic advice will enable teachers and those responsible for staff development both to identify the causes of stress, and to formulate a whole school policy for its management within the school.

Sue Ralph and Marie Brown both teach in the University of Manchester School of Education. They lecture and research in Educational Management and Administration, and Education and the Mass Media, and run inservice courses for teachers and other professionals. They have researched and published extensively on the effects of stress on teachers.

Paperback, 128 pages, tables.

Managing the Primary School Budget

BRENT DAVIES & LINDA ELLISON

With the framework of the Local Management of Schools firmly in place, heads, staff and governors need to turn their attention to its implementation at the local school level.

This practical guide begins by establishing the key dimensions of LMS and reviews the nature of income and expenditure in the primary school. It moves on to a consideration of the way in which budgeting fits into school management development planning and examines the role of staff and governors in the process.

The book then adopts a step-by-step approach using a case study school to demonstrate how to go through the three key stages of budgetary review, planning and implementation. This will provide primary schools with a practical framework enabling them to manage their new-found financial responsibilities.

Brent Davies BA MSc is Director of the International Educational Leadership and Management Centre, University of Humberside and is an LMS adviser to a large number of local education authorities. He has provided LMS management training for over 1000 primary heads in differing LEAs. He is the author of *Local Management of Schools* and a large number of articles on delegated finance. He is joint author with Linda Ellison of *Education Management for the 1990s*.

Linda Ellison MSc is a Senior Lecturer in charge of Education Management at Leeds Metropolitan University. She is extensively involved with programmes of senior management training, particularly for heads and deputies in primary schools. She has also been involved in the provision of staff development on LMS in a variety of LEAs. She is joint author with Brent Davies of *Education Management for the 1990s*.

Paperback, 128 pages, tables.

Marketing the Primary School

An Introduction for Teachers and Governors

BRIAN HARDIE

Schools have always had an eye on their 'reputation' and standing within the local community. However, open enrolment and competition for pupil numbers following the 1988 Education Reform Act have put a much greater value on the relationship which schools need to have with both parents and pupils. Now, in order to increase — and even maintain — pupil numbers, schools will be under much greater pressure to market themselves effectively. The author, who has been running courses in marketing and reputation management for primary school heads, shows how the primary school can be successfully promoted, stretching precious resources to make the most of contacts with the local community. Contents: Preface, the school in its marketplace, reputation management, marketing the school, meeting the customer, the prospectus and other communications, handling the media, further reading, useful addresses, glossary, index.

Brian Hardie MA DLC is an Education Consultant and formerly Senior Lecturer in Education Management at Crewe + Alsager Faculty of the Metropolitan University of Manchester, where he ran courses in marketing and reputation management for primary school Heads. He is the author of *Evaluating the Primary School* (Northcote House, 1994).

'...tells head how to think the unthinkable... sound advice about things that good schools should have been doing for years...' *Times Educational Supplement.*

'The book works, as a handbook to be used and returned to as different activities are needed. The context and priority are right... the ingredients for the successful mix are right... the focus and presentation of the advice are simple and sharp.' *NAGM News.*

Paperback, 144 pages, illustrated.

Local Management of Schools

BRENT DAVIES & CHRIS BRAUND

Written by two consultants in this important field, this book meets the pressing need for an introductory handbook to help governors, teachers and parents get to grips with major new responsibilities now becoming mandatory. Readable and practical, the book spells out the new legislation and what it means, the new financial structure in secondary and primary schools, the new role of Head teachers and governors in delegated school management, and what it means for the future. Complete with case studies and suggested management exercises.

'The nine main chapters, each dealing with a different aspect, are easy to read, comparatively jargon-free, and gave me a very good overview of LMS.... This reference book will justify a place in any educational establishment because of its accessible information and advice.' *Junior Education.* 'Well favoured by the brevity/practicality formula, written with governors and parents in mind as well as teachers. It is strong on illustrative yet simple graphics and tables and does not shirk the consequences of falling numbers.' *Times Educational Supplement.*

Paperback, 96 pages, tables.

The School Library

ELIZABETH KING MA ALA

Written by a former Chairperson of the School Library Association, this book appraises the role of school libraries in a changing world — a world in which new ideas, new technology and new initiatives (and financial cutbacks) present a special challenge for the professional. 'A stimulating appraisal of the role of the school library in a changing educational world of cutbacks, information technology and educational reform.' *Junior & Middle School Education Journal.*

Paperback, 112 pages, illustrated.

The School Meals Service

NAN BERGER OBE FHCIMA

The importance of the school meals service is becoming better recognised today, following greater interest in diet and health, and the advent of privatisation and what it means for standards of service in the educational system. This new book meets the longstanding need for an introduction to—and defence of—the School Meals Service. Expert, readable and forthright, it reviews key health and management issues for everyone having a professional interest in children's welfare, from head teachers and governors to catering managers and educational administrators.

Contents: Foreword, acknowledgements, the beginnings, what the service is and does, the structure of the service, training, nutrition, organising the production of school meals, the stigma of the free school meal, the competition, the problem of midday supervision, the economics of the School Meals Service, the effects of the Education (No. 2) Act 1980, the role of the Government, the future of the School Meals Service, appendices (organisations, statistics, notes on Scotland and Northern Ireland), chronology, bibliography, index.

'Informative, thought-provoking and controversial.' *Lunch Times*. 'Maori-style cooking has not, to my knowledge, been much practised by our own School Meals Service, though no doubt ungrateful children would have their parents believe otherwise. The kind of folklore perception of school dinners is tackled in Nan Berger's School Meals Service. There is much more to the book than this, however, for it is a thorough and well documented history of the meals service, starting with its origins in the last century and moving on to recent traumas of privatisation and closure.' *Times Educational Supplement*. Nan Berger OBE FHCIMA is former Editor of the *National Association of School Meals Organisers Handbook* and *Hospitality* magazine.

Paperback, 144 pages, illustrated.